THE
(NON-INFLATABLE)

MONTY
PYTHON

~~TV~~
~~COMPANION~~

THE (NON-INFLATABLE)

MONTY PYTHON

~~TV COMPANION~~

by

Jim Yoakum

DOWLING PRESS, INC.
NASHVILLE, TENNESSEE

Cover Design by Jesse Marinoff Reyes
Interior Design by BookSetters

www.noninflatable.freeservers.com

CONTENTS

ACKNOWLEDGEMENTS

Over the course of this book's long and winding 12-year road trip toward publication, there have been many people who have helped, a few that have hindered, and many who have gone beyond the course of duty. I thank you all. Here are some of the people without whom none of this would have been possible. If you don't like this book, they share the blame:

Anne James; Ralph Camp; Alison Davies and all at Mayday Management; Roger Saunders; Python (Monty) Pictures; Jill Feldman; Rolling Stone Magazine; Nancy Lewis; "Legs" Larry Smith; Terry Gilliam; Dean Cole; The British Broadcasting Corporation; Spy Magazine; Jodi Block; Terry Jones; Jean Drysdale; MTV; David Sherlock; Douglas Adams; Carol Cleveland; Neil Innes; Michael Palin; John Tomiczek; Graham Chapman; Martin Lewis; PythOnline (www.pythonline.com); Bonni Hall; Hans ten Cate (www.dailyllama.com); all on alt.fan.monty-python; Kim Howard "Johnson"; Eric Idle; Duitch; Jeanna Crawford; James Edgar; Alley Ernst and the Goring-on-Thames River-Widener's club who are a constant inspiration to those who follow useless pursuits every where.

To Michele, who inspires me.

A NOTE TO BUYERS OF THE NON-INFLATABLE EDITION

Just because you are a cheap buggar and have opted-out for the less expensive, shoddier, Non-Inflatable edition of this book, versus the larger, more complete, more expensive and infinitely nicer Inflatable edition, I want you to rest assured that this edition is exactly the same as the larger, more complete, more expensive and infinitely nicer Inflatable edition. Not one word has been expurgated! Not ~~one~~! What is more, buyers of this edition get something extra that buyers of the larger, more complete, more expensive and infinitely nicer Inflatable edition do not get: this page. *(That should make up for the fact that this edition is not as complete.)*

A LEGAL FOREWORD

What can one possibly say about *Monty Python* that has not already been the product of a major lawsuit? Evidently quite a lot, which is why you now hold this book in your hands. And quite a nice book it is too. I dare say that there are things in here that even I did not know, and I was there at the beginning, back when Monty Python was a mere niggling legal matter, and not the full-fledged lawsuit that it would eventually become.

Having said all that, I must admit that I have not, in a strict and legally-binding sense, actually read this book. However I have read the brief, and I feel certain that it will make a splendid lawsuit and live on in the courts for many years to come.

Graham Chapman
July 1988

'Somebody crack a
joke or something...'
An early group shot
from the 1st season.
From left: Terry
Jones, Graham
Chapman, Eric Idle,
Terry Gilliam,
Michael Palin and
John Cleese.

WHAT D'YA KNOW, THE REVOLUTION WAS TELEVISED!

This is not a fan's book (although I am a fan). Nor is this a stoic dissertation on *Monty Python* humor and its influence upon late 20th Century man. Those books and articles have already been written many times. This is a book about a social and cultural revolution as important in its impact as the storming of the Bastille or the advent of Beatlemania. This is the story of "a revolution in the head" that came to us disguised as a humorous television series called *Monty Python's Flying Circus.*

I first began work on this book in late 1986 because, after years of enjoying the *Monty Python* television shows and secretly thinking how hip I was to "get it all," I suddenly came to the crashing realization that I was still missing half the jokes. Sure, I snickered along with the best of them whenever a Python Pepperpot would nutter-on about "bleedin' Lord Hill," but it was a hollow chuckle. The truth was, I had absolutely no idea who Lord Hill was or what made him so damn funny in the first place. That's when I decided some serious investigation was in order, and I set out to discover more about people like Reginald Maudling, Lord Hill, and Mary Whitehouse – cultural references continually ticked off in Monty Python, and names that never failed to produce gales of laughter from the studio audience. The more I investigated, the more I learned about the workings of the British Broadcasting Corporation, the prevailing British social attitudes of the times, and even the backgrounds of the group themselves – the more I realized that to truly enjoy the Monty Python television shows one needs to have more than just a well-developed sense of the absurd, one needs to understand (or at least be aware) of the times and circumstances in which the shows were written, produced, and viewed.

When I first got the inspiration to write this book in late 1986, I did so because I had given up hopes of ever reading one like it. It's hard to remember in this "information-in-a-minute" modem-mad modern world, but less than 10 years ago it was very difficult to find any book by or about the Pythons, as most of them were either long out of print or else hard-to-find imports. In the decade since I wrote this book we have seen not only an impressive rise in the amount of books on the Pythons (thanks Kim!), but also a rise in the amount of books by the Pythons. We have seen the birth of a Python web site (www.pythonline.com) as well as an incredible explosion in the marketing of Monty Python merchandise (something that many members had fought against in the past). **After all these years, in the pages of all those books and web sites, I have yet to discover a book quite like this one.** I hope that it will both entertain and inform you.

On a personal note, I'd like to add that this book would not have been possible at all without the help and encouragement of the late Graham Chapman. Graham and his family (the late John Tomiczek and David Sherlock) took me into their home, their hearts and their confidences, and for that I will always be grateful. I am further grateful to the still-very-much alive David Sherlock, Graham's better half for many years, for his continued support and friendship. In 1997 I was honored to be named by David as Director of the Graham Chapman Archives, and as Literary Executor of the estate. It will be the duty of the Archives not only to preserve and protect Graham's life and work, but to also keep his name alive (even if he isn't) and his work before the public.

—Jim Yoakum January, 1999
www.noninflatable.freeservers.com

NOTE:

Aside from a Pythongraphy, this book deals strictly with the 5 year period (1969-1974) in which the Monty Python Flying Circus series was conceived, written, and produced.

Pre-Python. David Jason, Michael Palin, Terry Jones and Eric Idle in a publicity still for Do Not Adjust Your Set, a tea-time children's show that also featured The Bonzo Dog (Doo-Dah) Band.

ABOUT THE BBC

To try and explain the inner workings of any large corporation is daunting task, but to try and explain the inner workings of a large government controlled corporation is perhaps an impossible one. Still, to better understand some of the motives behind the actions of people like Lord Hill, it is best to know a little something about the British Broadcasting Corporation.

The BBC (or sometimes the Beeb, or "Auntie Beeb") is a major public institution, and one of the country's only means of communicating with its people. It is commercial free, and in that way it can be compared to Public Broadcasting in America, but the difference lies in that PBS is privately funded for the most part and, consequently, is not subject to the same intense pressures from "interested parties" as is the BBC. The "interested parties" with the most clout are, of course, the political ones. And while they don't like to appear (while in office) to be manipulating the Beeb, they do have one rather crude weapon that they swing over its head to ensure that Broadcasting House doesn't go too far: the license fee.

Now we come to one of the fundamental differences between American and British television: the British viewing audience is charged an annual fee to watch TV (radio is free). This fee is set by the government and administered by the Post Office, and is the only form of revenue the BBC has apart from syndication and merchandising sales. While it is one of the cheapest services in

Europe, a rise in the fee (essentially a tax) is always an unpopular political move; yet it is one that the politicians in power are willing to make – as long as the BBC behaves itself. If it doesn't, well, you get the picture (Then again, maybe you won't get the picture).

During most of the 1960s the BBC was expanding. People were buying TV sets at a steady pace and, along with the introduction of color TV, this meant that it was relatively free of economic pressure. But by the late '60s this expansion was over. Inflation was rising, causing the BBCs' cost to rise, and they were finding it increasingly difficult to survive on their current revenue. Clearly something had to be done.

The BBC is controlled by a group known as the BBC Board of Governors. These are highly distinguished private individuals who are appointed to the post by the government. It is their job to oversee the activities of the Director-General and the Board of Management. The BBC Board of Governors is headed by the Chairman, who is appointed directly by the Prime Minister. The BBC as a whole comes under the jurisdiction of the Home Secretary, who during this time was Reginald Maudling.

Just as the BBC is under pressure from politicians, they in turn are subject to pressures from other "interested parties" – lobby groups. The most celebrated of these special interest groups was the National Viewers' and Listeners' Association headed by a middle-aged ex-schoolteacher from Shropshire named Mrs. Mary Whitehouse, the original "Hell's Granny."

Mary Whitehouse first became concerned about the influence of broadcasting on public morality in the early 1960s. She was a committed Christian and a former supporter of Moral Rearmament (an early British version of the Reverend Jerry Falwell's Moral Majority). She was all in a twist about the secular attitude towards the family in schools and their morally neutral stance towards sex education. These declining moral values she attributed to the changed moral attitudes portrayed on television.

On May 5th, 1964, she and a like-minded woman, Mrs. Norah Buckland, held a rally at Birmingham Town Hall on the subject of declining moral values on television and, with virtually no organization, they managed to fill the hall to capacity. Their simple message was Clean Up TV. On March 16th, 1965, a more formal organization, the National Viewers' and Listeners' Association, was launched with Mary Whitehouse as Secretary.

In May 1967 they staged their first convention, and with the support of Malcolm Muggeridge (the host of the religious discussion program bumped to make room for Python) they formed a spin-off group called the Nationwide Festival of Light. **It was clear that Mary Whitehouse was a woman with entirely too much free time on her hands.**

The classic shot.
From left: Eric
Idle, Graham
Chapman, John
Cleese, Terry
Gilliam, Terry Jones
and Michael Palin

MONTY PYTHON'S FLYING CIRCUS

On the evening of October 5th, 1969, England was once again attacked from the air by the Flying Circus. Only, this time around it wasn't Baron Von Richtofen's, but *Monty Python's Flying Circus* that was inflicting all the damage. This flying circus dropped jokes instead of munitions, and there wasn't a single bomb in the bunch. To some viewers, being confronted by *Monty Python's Flying Circus* that evening was probably a bit of a shock – they'd been expecting to see a religious discussion program. No doubt they were also confused by the fact that not one person on the program appeared to be named Monty Python. From the first frame of the opening titles it was clear that they were (to borrow a soon to be familiar phrase) in "for something completely different." Cartoon violence, killer jokes… this wasn't the hip British satire of *Beyond the Fringe,* nor was it the comfortably corny vaudeville of Morcambe and Wise – this was… subversive! This was absurd! Silly! Something Completely Different! It was immediately relegated to cult status by the BBC, who buried it with irregular late night transmissions and virtually no publicity.

The program's format was a puzzler too. Gone were the conventions of normal sketch comedy with their mundane premises and punch lines, and in their place was a show that seemed not so much structured as strung together. Ideas and in-jokes spilled one on top of another in the crazy-quilting style of a daydream. Sketches could (and did) end unexpectedly, or without a punch line altogether. And lush, pretentious build-ups could lead to nothing more than the introduction of the next sketch. One episode contained enough ideas to sustain a hundred series, yet they were being burped out here at a rate of 20 per second.

The Pythons were pushing at the boundaries of conventional comedy and were finding that they weren't the insurmountable mountains they'd expected, but mere molehills.

Monty Python was a landmark series in the history of television. As Bob Hope was to comedy in the '40s, and Lenny Bruce in the '50s, *Monty Python* was the line of demarcation of a generation. They were the harbingers of a new set of laugh lines that declared "From now on, this is what's funny." They would deny this of course. They have said that they didn't set out to shatter the conventions of comedy, that their only goal was to be funny. But the Pythons were a product of their times, and their times (the late 1960s) were calling for humor that, as John Cleese has said, did more than "make jokes about the price of fish" (Although they could and did make jokes about the price of an albatross). Often misunderstood, and never far out of the spotlight of controversy, Python spearheaded what they called the "silly school" of humor, modeled more on the absurdities of *The Goon Show* rather than the satiric bite of *Beyond The Fringe* (their immediate predecessors), and it's for this reason that Python humor survives today. Silly, it seems, knows no era. Not for them the heavy-handed lampoonings of *That Was The Week That Was*, which mocked and satirized the current atmosphere of the time, rather Python "sent-up" and mocked current modes of thought. *Monty Python* was funny alright, but it was funny about ideas. Perhaps it was this very style of humor which led to many of their troubles, for it goes far beyond poking fun at the price of fish and attacks the very core of why we laugh, and what we laugh at.

By avoiding the temptation to be topical (like *That Was The Week That Was* and, in America, The Smothers Brothers) their shows withstand repeated viewings and are as fresh today as they were 30 years ago. *Monty Python's Flying Circus* set a new standard for humor, the reverberations of which can still be felt today in the style and attitudes of shows like *Saturday Night Live, The Young Ones, SCTV, It's Garry Shandling's Show, South Park, Beavis & Butthead, The Daily Show, Late Night with David Letterman* and *Not Necessarily The News;* as well as in the humor of comics like Emo Phillips, Steven Wright, Jim Carrey, Brian Regan, Robin Williams, Chip Chinnery, and the late Andy Kaufman. For better or worse (depending upon your view) it is mainly due to Monty

Python that what was once shocking is now regular prime time fare. While Python helped to define their (and our) age, they are not prisoners of it, for as long as there are overbearing authoritarians, inane TV chat shows, and calculating politicians – there will be men who dress as mice, flying sheep, and jokes that have the power to kill. In the end there is no situation that a healthy shouting of "Dinsdale!" can't improve.

The story of *Monty Python's Flying Circus* is one of accidents, calculations, inertia, bullying, apathy, enthusiasm, ignorance, intelligence, censorship, and unbridled imagination. It's the story of one television series and six men who, if not for varying degrees of all of the above, would have become doctors, lawyers, historians, advertising executives, English professors and, perhaps, politicians (For several years Cleese was quite vocal for the Social Democratic Party).

It's the story of six extremely individual individuals whose only common bond appeared to be the desire to make people laugh, and it's the story of the most influential and exciting comedy series of the last 50 years.

The Author
strikes a
jaunty
pose.

THE FIRST SERIES

"IT'S. . ."

A rare shot of the five surviving American Presidents. From left: Gerald R. Ford, Jimmy Carter, Ronald R. Reagan, George W. Bush and Bill Clinton.

Picture of the Royal Family, singing along as they watch "The Lumberjack Song" sketch

THE FIRST SERIES

Oct. 5, 1969 – Jan. 11, 1970

In 1969 one of the most popular television shows in America was *Green Acres*. In an era when Charlie Manson stalked the Hollywood hills and Charlie Company hacked their way along the Ho Chi Minh trail every night on the national news, was it any wonder that we followed the Dadaesque exploits of Oliver and Lisa Douglas and a talking pig named Arnold? America needed a good laugh. We were ready for *Monty Python's Flying Circus*. Too bad we had to wait five more years to get it.

In 1974 America was still in need of a good laugh. We were standing in line for gasoline, inflation was running rampant, and the only bright spot on the tube seemed to be Nixon's eminent resignation speech. Ron Devillier, a young Program Director for KERA-TV, a Dallas, Texas PBS station, was also looking for a good laugh. He was also looking for new programming. It was when he ambled into the Time-Life archives (the BBC distributor in America) in New York that he found both; for there on a shelf sat dozens of dusty video tapes labeled *Monty Python's Flying Circus*. His curiosity piqued, he watched one. Then he watched another. Then he ordered 26 episodes and flew back to Dallas with a big smile pasted on his face. America was about to laugh again.

Britain in the latter half of the 1960s could be a dismal place. The glittery trappings of the "Swinging London" set had long since rotted away, like the cheap, but flashy suits that had been hawked on Carnaby Street, revealing the bandy-kneed, spotty-bummed body of a country fast heading for the grim realities of major industrial reform. It was almost as if the "glory years" (actually little more than a year) of the mid-sixties had all been a dream; the incessant American tourists, the working class pop stars, the unblinking spotlight of the world's press – it was all but gone. Had England really won the World Cup? For the tiny island previously thought of as merely quaint and dowdy, it was a dream come true. Suddenly it was Quant, not quaint, as its eccentricities were elevated into High Style. England basked in its new-found prominence as a fashion mecca, and in the abnormally bright summer that accompanied it; but no sooner had it learned to cope with its new identity than its 15 minutes of fame were whisked away – leaving a gaping hole in both its spirit and its economy.

It was now 1969. The pound, which had been devalued two years previously, was at a low ebb, inflation was galloping across the continent, and British troops had just been sent that April to quell a weekend of street fighting among Catholics, Protestants, and the police in Belfast, Northern Ireland. Britain needed a good laugh. Early in May of that year six young rebels gathered together at the Light of Kashmir, an Indian restaurant in Fleet Road, London, and discussed secret plans over a curry. It had all the earmarks of a clandestine operation, only these anarchists weren't mad IRA bombers, rather British comedians – although ultimately the goals were the same: they planned to blitz England – with a non-stop barrage of humor – and bring her begging to her knees. The six young men (all between the ages of 25 and 30) were the six member of *Monty Python's Flying Circus:* Graham Chapman, John Cleese, Terry Gilliam, Eric Idle, Terry Jones, and Michael Palin.

At the start of 1969 there had been no group. Graham Chapman and John Cleese, who had been writing partners since their early Cambridge days, were busy scripting a myriad of projects, among which was *The Frost Report* and the odd episode of *Doctor In The House*, a medical comedy based on the popular books by Richard Gordon. They were also starring along side Marty Feldman in *At Last The 1948 Show.* Meanwhile, Michael Palin and Terry Jones (who were also partners), along with Eric Idle, were pre-occupied with writing and performing in *Do Not Adjust Your Set*, a children's television show that was also quite popular with adults because of its freewheeling comedy style and the mad musical contributions of the brilliant Bonzo Dog (Doo-Dah) Band. (Led by future Rutle, Neil Innes.) Cleese and Chapman would often wind-down their day by watching it, and after a viewing one afternoon they decided that "it was time to do more telly."

Cleese and Palin were the first to meet (although they all had a passing acquaintance of each other as writers on *The Frost Report*). Palin then brought in Jones, who brought in Idle, who brought in American animator Terry Gilliam. Gilliam also worked on *Do Not Adjust Your Set* and had long ago featured Cleese in a fumetti-style comic strip called "Christopher's Punctured Romance' when he'd worked as Associate Editor for Harvey (Mad) Kurtzman's short-lived comic magazine, *Help!*, in New York (The strip involves Cleese's obsession with a Barbie doll). The group discussed the current state of comedy and the type of comedy program that they would like to do. Together they approached Barry Took, a writer and producer at the BBC, about doing such a show, and he in turn sold the idea to the executives at the Light Entertainment Department. Took had been acting as a sort of talent scout for the BBC, and had been eyeing various writer/performers. Took: "In my mind's eye I put together a team of four (later to become six) which were John Cleese and Graham Chapman and Michael Palin and Terry Jones. They used to meet, and argue, at my house, and then they'd all go home and call me up throughout the evening, asking if I thought they were ruining their careers joining it with this New Thing!" On May 23, 1969, all six Pythons, along with directors Ian MacNaughton and John Howard Davies, met with Michael Mills, the BBC's Head of Comedy. He promptly commissioned them to write and perform a 13-part series, without so much as demanding a pilot, and left the room. It was only the second time the six Pythons had all sat together in the same room. "That's how it was in those days," recalls Jones. " 'Right, thirteen shows then!' It's all terribly changed now." John Cleese: "When you look back, it really was an amazing act of courage on the part of the BBC to go straight to series without demanding a pilot. I mean, I really was the only one who had been on much, as a performer. I will always thank the BBC for that."

Monty Python's Flying Circus happened-along during the close of a rather unusual time at the BBC, a period of unrestrained freedom and creative carte blanche. **It was a period when "Auntie Beeb" really kicked up her heels and let her hair down; She became "with it" and relevant and quite, quite outspoken**. Gone was the stodgy image and narcoleptic programming, and in their place sat gritty police dramas like *Z Cars* and realistically drawn human shows like *Cathy Come Home*, shows that painted a grimmer portrait of Wilson's Britain than the one he chose to exhibit. The man responsible for this "new attitude for 'Auntie'" was a rather amazing individual named Sir Hugh Carlton-Greene. Sir Hugh (brother of writer Graham Greene) was Director-General of the BBC, and that rarest of animals – an executive with common sense. He believed that the "best ideas come from below, not from above," and allowed an unprecedented nine-year period of creativity to exist and develop at the BBC; simply leaving people alone to "get on with it." Unfortunately for the Pythons, they were just beginning to "get on with it" when Sir Hugh retired (was pushed out, some contend) on March 31, 1969. And while the group was to enjoy a brief period of creative expansion after Sir Hugh's exodus, the BBC was fast entering an era of creative contraction.

This contraction was due to many factors, chief among them being the appointment of Lord Hill to the position of Chairman for the BBC Board of Governors. Lord Hill (famous as *The Radio Doctor* in the 1940s) had previously been Chairman of the Independent Television Authority (now the IBA), which supervises the activities of Britain's commercial television companies. While there is no hard evidence that Hill had been appointed by Prime Minister Wilson to do "a hatchet job" on the BBC for any real or imagined slights (Hill denied that he was), it was no secret that there was little love lost between the BBC and Independent Television. There was also little love lost between Lord Hill and Sir Hugh Carlton-Greene. Upon his arrival at Broadcasting House, Hill immediately began to isolate and compartmentalize. Perhaps it's mere coincidence, but it was only months after Hill's appointment that Carlton-Greene retired.

His vacancy left Hill (hardly a pioneering liberal) free to cast a more discerning eye over the Beeb's more "problemistic" programs, Monty Python being chief among them. Hill had been a "hands on" chairman at ITA, a tradition he intended to uphold at the BBC.

There was also pressure from Mrs. Mary Whitehouse, an ex-Shropshire schoolteacher and her National Viewers' and Listeners' Association (or National VALA as she like to refer to it, preferring to play on the acronym). National VALA was a media watchdog organization formed in 1964 in an effort to keep an eye on broadcasting's influence on public morality. Her Clean Up TV campaign was gaining support throughout the nation, and she was fast becoming a voice to be reckoned with. Lord Hill received a delegation from National VALA (unlike Greene), and so it was with a self-satisfied feeling of accomplishment that she wrote: "With Lord Hill at the BBC, sharper eyes will be focused on the scripts." An understatement to be sure.

It was against this backdrop of creative implosion/explosion that the first series of Monty Python got underway, the first order of business being to decide what to name the new series. Graham Chapman: "We were all busy trying to write the first 13 episodes of the series, and weren't desperately keen on spending a lot of time arguing about titles: there'd already been suggestions, things like *Owl Stretching Time, The Toad Elevating Moment, Sex and Violence...* and Terry Jones came up with a nice one which was *A Horse, A Bucket, and a Spoon.* I must say I rather liked – never understood – but rather liked that one." Their first impulse was to have the show go out under a different title each week, but cooler heads at the BBC prevailed (Actually they were trying to avoid the headache involved with such an idea as costumes would be logged under one title, makeup under another and so on). "Eventually," Graham Chapman stated, "the Head of Comedy (Michael Mills) came into our shed and told us that he wouldn't let us leave until we'd given him a title, and that it had to have the word 'circus' in it as it had appeared on various contracts and interdepartmental memos. See, the BBC had loosely referred to the six of us wandering around the building as 'a circus' - a kind of BBC joke, tee hee - and so we added 'flying' to it to make it sound less like a real circus, and more like something to do with the First World War, then added "Monty Python" because he sounded like a really bad theatrical agent — just the sort of guy who might have got us together. None of us liked it, but none us hated it, so it was a typical committee decision, really." Terry Jones remembers it (of course) differently. Terry Jones: "It wasn't *A Horse, A Bucket, and a Spoon*, it was *A Horse, A Spoon, and A Basin*. Well, that's what I remember, and anyway, I'm sure it was Graham who came up with it and not me. But things do get a bit misty. *The Toad Elevating Moment* was Graham's, and was a favorite of mine-although it never stood a chance."

Ian MacNaughton says "we chose the title for three carefully considered reasons: because as far as we knew there was no one named Monty Python, because it had nothing to do with flying and because it was not a circus."

According to Jones, the name "Monty Python" actually sat with them for several weeks before finally being decided upon, thus leaving such titles as *BB Circus, Gwen Dibley's Flying Circus, Arthur Megapode's Cheap Show, The Atomic Circus* and *Valeline Review* to the dustbin of history. (Although a lot of abandoned titles like *The Ant: An Introduction and Sex and Violence* appeared at the end of first series episodes as subtitles. The group has an admitted difficulty in deciding on what to name things. A similar situation arose when trying to find a name for *Monty Python's Life of Brian*.)

John Cleese is having problems with his parrot in "The Parrot Shop" sketch (Series 1, Episode 8)

Also foremost in the minds of the group (Palin and Jones especially) was the overall feel and format of the show. Jones had been inspired by Spike (*The Goon Show*) Milligan's Q series which had a tendency to abandon punch lines, stop sketches in the middle, and had an ever-expanding line of lateral thinking where characters from one sketch could spill over into another until the whole mess became so muddled that Milligan would wander off the set mumbling "Who wrote this?" Jones: "Milligan just ripped out all form and shape. He'd start a sketch which turned into another sketch which turned again into something else. I thought 'shit, he's done it!' Another inspiration had been an animation Gilliam had done for *Do Not Adjust Your Set* called "Elephants" It was really a prototype for his Python animations with their absurd premises and point-of-reference narratives. Jones felt that this tumbling stream-of-consciousness style could help some of their more eccentric comedy bits work. Palin and Gilliam readily agreed, as did Idle, and while Chapman and Cleese were less concerned with the overall feel as much as they were the individual sketches, they also agreed, feeling that this style would allow them to explore more unusual areas of comedy.

Although much is made of this stream-of-consciousness style and the abandonment of punch lines, a close study of the first series proves it to be much more sketch-oriented than surreal. **This is because they had an enormous back log of rejected sketch material that, while good, had been decided to be "too stupid, to silly, too rude" for the programs that they had originally been written for**. "They won't understand that in Bradford" was the usual stock reply, sort of the British version of the American "But will it play in Peoria?" excuse. Oddly enough, one of the sketches ("The Mouse Problem") had been rejected by none other than Marty Feldman as being too "weird."

The director they chose to work with (or was chosen for them by Michael Mills) was Ian MacNaughton, who had also directed Milligan's Q series. MacNaughton was a burly Scotsman with a keen eye for locations and a demented sense of humor that quickly endeared him to most of the Pythons (although Idle and Cleese seemed less fond of him), but prior commitments to the BBC limited his early work with the group to only directing the filmed inserts on the first four programs while John Howard Davies handled the direction on the studio portions (MacNaughton still occasionally works with the group, his last project being on *Monty Python Live At the Hollywood Bowl.* He presently lives in Germany).

In the beginning the group was a little cautious with each other (after all, they were virtual strangers) and were careful to put their best foot forward at all times. Chapman and his longtime companion, David Sherlock, decided that a little "get acquainted" session was in order, and so that summer all six Pythons and their mates bundled off to Henley-on-Thames for an impromptu picnic. This event proved to be a fortuitous occasion for both television comedy and the food industry, as it led to the development of some of the most bizarre characters ever to appear on the TV screen - the Pepperpots. Earlier in the day Chapman and Sherlock had decided to visit a little tea shop in Hampstead to buy some supplies, and while there they spotted the owners of the shop, a gaggle of elderly women, camped behind the counter laboring away with their brand new electric cash register. They watched in amusement as one would ring up the purchases on the electric till while calling them out to another who would methodically write them down in a shaky hand on a scrap of paper. David Sherlock explains: "These mad creatures were checking the automatic till by hand, which would take twice as long, because they didn't trust it…all the while chatting away…this led to many of the Pepperpotty ideas."

The picnic also had a profound effect on Michael Palin, for it was the first time he'd ever tasted Helmann's Mayonnaise, real mayonnaise being something of a luxury in England at the time. It stunned him to such an extent that, in his culinary lust, he visited the little tea shop later to purchase some and it was there that he experienced the Pepperpots first hand. An idea exploded. From such humble origins are these things sometimes born.

Although they soon discovered that they had the makings of an unbelievable partnership, they still tended to huddle about in the same comfortable writing groups as before: Chapman and Cleese, Palin with Jones, Idle and Gilliam alone. It is not as well known that Terry Gilliam fancied himself as a writer. His animation style was certainly influential to the overall shaping and tone of the show, but it was as a writer that he first approached Humphrey Barclay (producer of *Do Not Adjust Your Set*) for a job in 1968.

Gilliam had appeared in England the previous year (to avoid appearing in Vietnam) and soon landed several freelance illustration jobs for various London magazines, but he quickly tired of this and asked old pal John Cleese if he couldn't help him land a job in television. Cleese suggested that he call Barclay. It is reported that Barclay was underwhelmed by Gilliam's written sketches (although he bought two) and that it was only when Gilliam mentioned that he was also a cartoonist that Barclay perked up (Barclay was also a cartoonist, his work having previously appeared in *Varsity*, the Cambridge University undergraduate newspaper). Gilliam was hired on the spot to do the odd animation for *Do Not Adjust Your Set,* and the rest is history. (Lest we have Barclay's less-than-amused reaction color our views on Gilliam's talents as a writer, we should be reminded that he is credited as co-author on most of his post-Python films, including *Time Bandits, Brazil, The Adventures of Baron Munchausen,* and *Fear And Loathing In Las Vegas.* By the same token, the rest of the group, especially Cleese, used to kid Gilliam about his use of the English language which they say was, well, limited. Cleese used to claim that Gilliam's vocabulary stretched to about 30 words).

Gilliam admits that he didn't know the first thing about animation (except what he'd read) when he suggested to the frazzled producer of *We Have Ways of Making You Laugh* that a problem sketch of his might be better presented as an animated film. Suddenly he found himself with a $1000 budget and a two-week deadline. Faced with these restrictions he decided that the only form of animation that would work, and the only type that he could do, was cut-out animation. He took photocopies of figures from old magazines and books (Sears Roebuck catalogs from the early 1900s seemed to work best), cut them out, put them on a drawing board and took their picture. Then he moved the figures a fraction of an inch and took their picture again. It took all two weeks to produce two minutes of film. This cut-out style, with its herky-jerky movements, suited perfectly the Gilliam personality. It suggested crude, coarse, Punch and Judy style humor replete with lavatorial and scatological references. It's a style of humor Gilliam is attracted to, and a style that also seemed to spill over into his first post-Python film, *Jabberwocky,* although he claims that he was just being true to the historical period.

Within Python, Gilliam's films served as a bridge between sketches, and as an escape route from ideas that didn't quite end. "There would be sketches," Gilliam said, "and when they ran out of steam they would say, 'Gilliam takes over and gets us from here to there.' It was a wonderful way to work." He calls the two-and three week sessions required to make each short film "brain damaging work" and admits that it wasn't very disciplined. He had desk drawers at his studio crammed full of photographs of arms, skies, noses, feet, buildings, and knees. Often an idea suggested itself merely because, in the jumble, a certain cut-out was positioned on another. He is also quick to defend himself by saying that he never damaged the source books themselves, but that he always cut out photocopies. "I have too much respect for books to do that," he says.

Gilliam often pulled seven day work weeks, with at least two all-nighters, in order produce a film, and when the work was all done he'd throw a blanket over his head and record the sound effects. When taping time came at Television Center, Gilliam would arrive with a can of film under his arm and the rest of the group would view his contribution to the show — along with the studio audience. Like it or not, that was what they were going to have to use. **Gilliam's freedom within the group structure was unparalleled, and he faced very few restrictions - mainly because no one ever knew what he was going to do beforehand, least of all himself.** The only act of full censorship for a Gilliam cartoon was one of self-censorship, when he decided that a first series animation of a telephone engineer working on a telegraph pole was a step too close to the edge — especially since it's revealed that the pole is, in reality, one of the three crosses of Calvary. Gilliam: "Taking something out of context gives me more pleasure than anything else." The Gilliam vocabulary may be limited , but it seems that the Gilliam imagination knows no such boundaries. Terry Gilliam's animations were as important in setting the tone of *Monty Python's Flying Circus* as was the writing; consequentially, so are knowing his influences. Artistically they include Hieronymous Bosch, Dali, and Max Ernst, as well as the innovative comedy of Ernie Kovacs. He also shares an admiration for Buster Keaton with Terry Jones, the other directing Python, especially his film classic, Sherlock Junior.

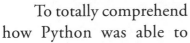

Terry Gilliam Artwork—
Show Titles

To totally comprehend how Python was able to spring, fully developed, onto the TV screen it's important to understand the group's influences, comic and otherwise. For Michael Palin these include the Arthurian legend, trains and Spike Milliagan. Terry Jones lists poetry, Chaucer and *The Goon Show*. John Cleese liked American sitcoms from the '50s like *Sergeant Bilko* and *Amos n' Andy* along with *The Goon Show*. Graham Chapman was keen on *The Footlights, The Goon Show,* and medicine, whereas Eric Idle makes a point of saying *The Goon Show* never meant much to him, that he like *Beyond The Fringe,* the theatre and music.

It's odd that Idle, an acknowledged "word freak," was not enamored of The Goons and the thesaurian prattle that was characteristic of chief Goon,

Spike Milligan. Still, *Beyond The Fringe* was no linguistic lay-about either, not with the late Peter Cook (declared by Idle to be "the funniest man in the world") in there to stir things up.

Although they shared many of the same mentors, Cleese bemoans the fact that the group didn't spread out more and write with different partners within the group. (No doubt wishing to stave-off the "low threshold of boredom" for which he is so rightly famous.) But he may have been speaking only for himself, for the group did exchange partners occasionally (Chapman proving to extremely versatile), and they even wrote sketches in whole committee.

A scene from the 'Double Vision Mountaineer' sketch. One of the only sketches written by the team of Eric Idle and John Cleese.

AS far as writing styles are concerned, it can be safely assumed that any sketch that features acts of abuse and doing strange things to small animals was written by Cleese and Chapman. Anytime you see a man with an odd disability, such as The Butcher Whose First Answer Is Always A Rude One, or see a man who chatters on about "some useless information that's supposed to fire our imagination," then it was probably written by Eric Idle (or Jagger/Richards). A lush, slow pan across a beautiful vista that ultimately reveals nothing more than a nude man seated at an organ is more than likely a Palin/Jones concoction. But there are no hard and fast rules. Idle could do abuse ("The Batley Townswomen's Guild's Re-enactment of the Battle of Pearl Harbor"), Cleese and Chapman could do wordplay ("Shunt's Utopia") or else they could team-up and do a deliberate parody of one of the other's style ("A day In The Life Of An Ordinary Stockbroker" which paired Chapman and Idle mocking a typical Palin and Jones sketch).

The team-writers had their own usual method for putting things down on paper. The method that Cleese and Chapman preferred was for Cleese to visit Chapman at home, or vice-versa, usually arriving at about 10 o'clock in the morning (Chapman claimed that he was usually about 30 minutes late, even when they met at his house). They would then sit around and chat, drink coffee and do the crosswords – basically do anything to avoid that awful moment when they had to put something funny down on paper. If their method proved to be too effective, and nothing funny ever came to them, they would, as their final tactic, attack Roget's Thesaurus and merely stare at words. This usually sparked-off some idea ("The Ministry of Silly Walks" came this way), but, if by noon nothing happened they would give up and go to lunch. Palin and Jones had a bit more unusual arrangement in that they'd work together – in separate houses. No one is too sure exactly how it worked, but it did, so they left it alone. All material then had to be presented before the group at a writing-meeting and voted on for its inclusion. This was not an easy, or enviable, task as the individual Pythons could be the worst audience in the world; one that could withhold a laugh out of jealousy, temperament or just plain bad manners. It was, as Cleese has said, democracy gone mad, but, if a piece got laughs it was given three asterisks. If it got a reasonable amount of chuckles, but not total apoplexy, it got two, and if it only got a few titters it got one mark. No laughs at all guaranteed that the piece would either be reworked by the original author or an interested other party, or else be palmed-off on someone else, like David Frost. A conscious effort was made to keep the humor as generic as possible, not because they couldn't imitate the people of their times (they could), but rather because of money.

The BBC was parsimonious at best, and what little money they did get (They had a budget of about $6000 an episode) had to be split six ways, so they always bore in mind repeats – for repeats meant repeat fees. One look at the more topical comedy shows of the time, *Laugh-In* and early *Saturday Night Live*, proves what a wise move this was on the part of the Pythons. Today's topical fodder often becomes tomorrow's puzzled yawn. The writing-meetings were also the source of much consternation for the group, for tempers can run high when you have six extremely talented and extremely opinionated people barricaded in a little room fighting over their material. Sometimes things got a little nasty, like the time Jones threw a glass ashtray at Cleese during preliminary discussions for *Monty Python and the Holy Grail* (It missed its intended target). Terry Jones, for one, doesn't recall all that much discord between himself and John Cleese. Jones: "I sometimes feel I'm too up-close and haven't got enough distance (on Python). It's why I didn't realize what was going on in the group dynamics until many years after the TV shows. But then, I'm always like that."

But the voting could be the tensest time, for each member had, almost as a secret weapon, the "writer's veto." The writer's veto could be used at any time, by any member of the group, whenever they felt that a sketch had gone too far. It could be used out of jealousy. Although it was never officially vetoed-out, Terry Jones expressed initial concern about a Cleese/Chapman sketch called "The Undertakers". The sketch involved a man (Cleese) who brings his dead mother, in a sack to an undertaker (Chapman) who suggests that they eat her. Jones' concern wasn't over the humorous quality of the sketch for he laughed himself silly (Gilliam laughed so hard that he was out of commission for the rest of the day), but rather it was concern over the sensibilities of his elderly parents. Funny won the battle though, and the sketch escaped unharmed.

Voting also had certain disadvantages for Idle and Gilliam, for as solo writers they only got one vote apiece while the teams could fight together for their work. More often than not Gilliam's main role at these writing-meetings was as a tiebreaker in the voting process. He quickly discovered that it was hopeless to try and read out his animations to the group, as most of their humor lay the grunts and groans that accompanied them and all he would receive from the others were polite smiles (Cleese often found Gilliam's work either brilliant, or else it would really piss him off). Sparring for their respective teams would usually be Terry Jones and John Cleese. You could not find two more dissimilar people than Terry Jones and John Cleese. Jones is small, Welsh, Oxford educated, with a voice that tends to rise a few octaves when he's excited about something, while Cleese is well over six feet, British and petulant. He is the more structured comedian who feels all comedy must maintain an internal logic at all times, that is, if you've got three men dressed as bananas and another man enters not dressed as a banana, you'd better have a damn good reason as to why not. Jones is a much more instinctive writer who believes in letting his imagination roam where it may, no explanations needed. It also didn't help matters that he had a background in mime. Cleese, Chapman and Idle had a distinct anti-mime bias at the time, a feeling they gave vent to in the last show of the first series where Chapman portrays a man who first mimes being hit on the head with a 16-ton weight – then actually is hit on the head with a 16-ton weight. Subtle stuff, indeed.

The Cleese/Jones confrontations made for heated exchanges, but while the Pythons disagree on nearly everything else, everyone agrees that these battles were for the general good of the show as they assured that only the best material was ever recorded. For the most part the team did all of their own acting, even going into drag to play a Pepperpot, although occasionally they used other actors in support roles. Most notable are Carol Cleveland (who played all the pretty girl parts and even appeared in the group's publicity stills for the first series), Connie Booth (Cleese's wife and future collaborator on *Fawlty Towers*) and *Do Not Adjust Your Set* script editor Ian Davidson. Oddly, Terry Gilliam makes very few appearances during the first series (certainly not as many as made later on), although he was quite possibly busy with the animation, which he professes was nearly always last minute.

The majority of each episode was scripted (there was little time or money or ad libbing), a typed copy would be sent to the BBC and then they would get down to the serious business of role casting. Most of the roles were up for grabs, depending on who had the nerve to say "I want to play this", although height often played a part in casting. This meant that most of the authority roles (policeman, doctors, barristers) went to the tallest members of the group (Cleese and Chapman), while the madder roles, the inflamed short people roles, went to the others. Just because someone had written a sketch, that didn't mean that they automatically got to play the part: "Argument Clinic", "The Dead Parrot", "Pet Conversion"... all were written by Cleese and Chapman, all were played by Cleese and Michael Palin. A lot of this had to do with the fact that Chapman was a budding young alcoholic at the time and was less interested in the endless hours of rehearsing than he was in going off to the bar for a drink. Besides, he said that he felt the really important part was the writing.

(A word about Graham's drinking. Although Chapman's romance with alcohol was not yet the problem it would eventually become, it was already having an effect on his work. Eric Idle: "Graham was a very strange planet. Since he was drunk so much of the time he wasn't the most accurate observer of people. In fact, he was desperately paranoid, probably about his gayness amongst all those tweedy doctor–y types, so that's why he got so paralytic. Since he never said much– and wrote even less– it was never easy to know just exactly what he was thinking. When he sobered–up and straightened–out he was a wonderful chap.")

Several running and stock characters developed during the first series: The Colonel, The Gumbies, The Pepperpots, The City Gents, and, especially, The Hermit (or the "It's" Man). All of The Hermit's introduction segments ("It's...") for the first series were filmed at one time on location in Bradford ("They won't understand *that* in Bradford!") because Ian MacNaughton had a girlfriend there. All of the filmed inserts for the entire series were lensed in a three- to five- week period some two months before the studio portions were shot. This meant that they were writing a series a year before they did the next one, as all 13 had to be written well in advance to insure continuity. Each episode was then given 90 minutes to complete in the studio at Television Center before a live audience. They would do a sketch and, as they nipped off to change for the next bit, the audience was shown one of the cartoons or a filmed insert. This would then be pieced together in the editing room to form one complete episode. It was confusing, no doubt, for the studio audience, but the group (especially Cleese and Chapman) disdained the studio audience anyway, as they felt they only got in the way of

Pre-Python. David Sherlock and Graham Chapman at a party in their London flat, 1967. This picture was taken mere hours before the 'severance of the peonie' incident made famous in Graham's books 'A Liar's Autobiography' and 'Graham Crackers'

the punch lines. Their audience was the one at home, and so they paced their lines accordingly. (The group wanted to ditch the studio audience altogether, but the BBC wouldn't allow the show on the air without one. No doubt it was a holdover from the old radio days.)

The episodes were shown in a different order than they were recorded (a common practice) as this allowed the best shows to be shown first and last respectively. Most of the continuity of the series was shouldered by the linking process, a chore that they dislike at first as they felt it too reminiscent of the type of comedy they abhorred (The type that featured a man who stood in front of the camera and introduced sketches with stupid things like "Wouldn't it be funny if...?" or "Haven't you ever wondered what it would be like if..."). However the linking process soon proved to be the key to establishing the famed stream-of-consciousness style ("The Rehearsing Bishop" linking in the second series is a good example of creative linking, not for just one episode, but for the entire series), and they soon came to enjoy it a lot.

The choice of using John Phillip Sousa's "Liberty Bell March" as the series' theme music is clouded in mystery, although Gilliam believes it was the choice of Python production assistant Roger Last. It is forever ruined for the band of the Grenadier Guards as they can hardly ever play it without someone sniggering, or else half-expecting a large cartoon foot to come crashing down in the middle of bar 32 accompanied by a raspberry (The foot belongs to Cupid and was taken from Bronzino's painting *Venus and Cupid*).

The group doesn't recall any adverse reaction to the first series from the BBC. Ironically, it was the group that was the first to complain. Their gripes were not the lofty bitches about freedom and artistic license, but rather the more mundane grievances an actor has regarding publicity and transmission times. Often the show was pre-empted (usually by *The Horse of the Year Show*) and the only publicity they'd received in the *Radio Times* (the BBC TV guide) had been exretable, calling the show "zany, oddball" and "satirical" (Satire was the one form of comedy that they were working overtime to try and dismantle). But, aside from these complaints and, coupled with the fact that the Head of Light Entertainment, Tom Sloane, disliked the show intensely, the series that began principal shooting in August 1969 went out without a hitch. England, the group, and the world, would never be the same again.

A scene from 'Hell's Grannies', a spoof-type sketch typical of the 1st series.

THE EPISODES

The episodes are listed in chronological order of original transmissions, with original transmission date, number in order of recording (in brackets) and date of recording (also in brackets). The transmission order of the first three series was different from the order in which they were recorded so that the best shows could be placed first and last in the series.

A few sketches were transferred to a different show after they were edited, and some shows have a subtitle. In most cases these subtitles were rejected names for the series, but not always. The series were recorded in two marathon sessions, which accounts for the dual dates under series headings. Compiling a running order for *Monty Python's Flying Circus* has been compared to trying to make a set of blueprints for a surrealist painting; the shows hardly ever have sketches that begin and end in the traditional sense. Consequently the details below are merely indications as to the content of a sketch.

Principal animation links are indicated by an asterisk (*), and are occasionally given titles, but, as they are usually more surreal than the sketches, even the team themselves soon gave up any hope of describing them in their scripts and just indicated where they should go.

The shows were written and performed entirely by Graham Chapman, John Cleese (except most of the fourth series), Eric Idle, Terry Jones, and Michael Palin. Special appearances are made by Carol Cleveland, Connie Booth, and Mrs. Idle (Eric's first wife). Animations and occasional appearances are by Terry Gilliam.

Interesting trivia surrounding the writing, performing, or reception of a sketch is detailed in brackets {}at the end of each episode.

The author didn't send a caption for this one, so suffice it to say that it is of a bunch of people doing something funny in bonnets and straw hats.

FIRST SERIES

October 5, 1969 – October 26, 1969
November 23, 1969 – January 11, 1970

1: "Whither Canada?" October 5, 1969 (2) (September 7, 1969):
"It's Wolfgang Amadeus Mozart" (famous deaths) / "Italian Lesson
"*Whizzo Butter ad / "It's The Arts" – interview ('Do you mind if I call
you Edward?'), Arthur 'Two-Sheds' Jackson, Picasso riding a bicycle /
"*Sit up!", The funniest joke in the world.

For those curious who want to know what "the funniest joke in the world"
might be to the Pythons, you're in for disappointment. Although we
never hear an English-language version of the joke (no doubt for our own
safety) the joke in German goes like this:

"Wenn is dass nod-schtuck git un slottermeier?"
   "Ja, beyerhunt das oder die flipperwalt gershput!"
It is , of course, in pig-German and technically it translates as:
   "When is the now-peace (git a) slotterfarmer?"
   "Yes, German dog the or the flipperwalt gershput!"

2: "Sex And Violence" October 12, 1969 (1) (August 30, 1969):
"Flying sheep, French Professors Lecture on Sheep Aviation" / "A Man with Three Buttocks" / "A Man With Two Noses" / "Arthur Ewing and his Musical Mice" / "Naughty Marriage Counselor" / "The Wacky Queen" / "Working Class Playwright" / "A Scotsman on a Horse" / "The Wrestling Epilogue" / "*Killer Pram / "The Mouse Problem".

"The Wacky Queen" was cut from the repeat of August 25, 1970 and never reinserted. "The Mouse Problem" was a Cleese / Chapman sketch originally written for Marty Feldman's show, *Marty*, but was deemed to be too silly by Feldman. Also, in the official book of scripts (*Monty Python: All The Words*) there is a short sequence featuring the Amazing Kargol and Janet (an embryonic version of the more famous "Mystico and Janet") commenting on "The Mouse Problem" that has never appeared in the U.S. version of this sketch. In "The Wrestling Epilogue," Thom Jack is introduced as the author of *Hello Sailor*. Eric Idle later wrote a book by that title. Terry Jones, in his book *Chaucer's Knight*, noted that the joke in this sketch, about fighting to prove the existence of God, is the same one made by Geoffrey Chaucer nearly 600 years ago in the *Canterbury Tales*. Notice the enormous amount of people in this episode named Arthur. It was a favorite character name of Cleese and Chapman's in honor of Arthur Lowe, a British comic actor.

3: "How to Recognize Different Types of Trees From Quite a Long Way Away" October 19, 1969 (3) (August 14, 1969):
"How to Recognize Different Types of Trees from Quite a Long Way Away" (Number One: The Larch) / Court scene (Witness in coffin, Cardinal Richalieu) / The larch / "Bicycle Repairman" / Children's stories ('With a melon?') / Restaurant sketch / "*Tired of That Dull Life?" / "Seduced Milkman" / Stolen Newsreader / Children Identifying Trees / "Nudge Nudge, Wink Wink".

4: "Owl Stretching Time" October 26, 1969 (4) (September 21, 1969):

Song / "Art Gallery" (eating paintings) / "Art Critic" / "It's a Man's Life in the Modern Army" / "Self Defense Against Fresh Fruit" / "Bookshop", "Dentist / Spy".

5: "Man's Crises of Identity in the Latter Half of the 20th Century" November 16, 1969 (5) (October 3, 1969):

"Confuse-A-Cat" / "The Smuggler" (watch), "Discussion with a Duck a Cat and a Lizard" / "Vox Pops on Smuggling" / "Police Raid" (certain substances) / "Letters, Vox Pops" / "Newsreader arrested" / Erotic film / "*Body Building" / Silly interview / "Careers Advisory Board / "Burglar-Encyclopedia Salesman".

"Confuse-A-Cat" was a Cleese / Chapman sketch based on a real cat who lived next door to Chapman and David Sherlock in the Belsize Park area of London. This cat never appeared to move, and would only stare as its owner clipped the lawn all day. "Police Raid" was a none-too-subtle swipe at Detective Norman Pilchard, the real life "pop star cop" who made a career out of busting people like John Lennon and the Rolling Stones. Pilchard always carried a sizeable quantity of hashish on his person, just in case his victims forgot to bring their own evidence. Also note that his name here is Police Constable Henry Thatcher, another dig, this one at up-and-coming politico Margaret Thatcher. The "Vox Pop" section in this episode features the first-ever appearance of a Gumby, played by John Cleese.

6: November 23,1969 (7) (November 5, 1969):

*"Signature" / "It's The Arts" with Johann Gambolputty de von Ausfernschpledensclittcrasscrenbonfrieddiggerdingledangledongleburstein-vonknackerthrasherapplebangerhorowitzicolensicgranderkoknottyspelltin-klegrandlichgrumblemeyerspelterwasserkurstlichhimbleeeisenbahnwagengutenabend bitteeinnurnburgerbratwrstlegerspurtenmitzweimacheluberhundsfutgum-beraberschonendankeralbsfleischmittlerraucher Von Hauptkopf of Ulm / "Non-Illegal Robbery" / Vox pops / "Crunchy Frog" / "The Extremely Dull

Life of a City Stockbroker" / "Red Indian in the Theatre" / "Policeman Make Wonderful friends / "A Scotsman on a Horse (again)" / *"You'll Never Take Me Alive Copper" / 20th Century Vole, "Film Producer and Toadying Writers".

"Johann Gambolputty..." was remembered by Chapman as being one of his two worst memories of doing the series. His agony was due not only to the incredible name he had to remember, but also to the fact that the group had been booted out of their normal digs at Television Center and moved to a theatre for two episodes. "The Extremely Dull Life of a City Stockbroker" was a Chapman / Idle sketch that mocked a typical Palin / Jones sketch. They had written it as a joke, to see if anyone noticed, and were astonished when the group liked it and wanted to include it in the show. Sharp eyes will notice that the topless girl at the newsagents Cecile Mould, is the same one who performs the sped-up striptease in episode 11.

7: "You're No Fun Anymore" November 30, 1969 (6) (October 10,1969):

Camel spotting / "You're No Fun Anymore" / "The Audit" / "Science fiction Sketch", "Man Turns into Scotsman", "Police Station", "Podgorny", "Science Fiction".

This episode features an odd technique for the team, the use of blackouts. It harkens back to all of those bad "spoof" shows that they were trying so hard to dismantle. "The Science Fiction Sketch", lasting nearly the full half hour, was written mainly by Palin and Jones. It was one of their first efforts to move the team out of TV and into the longer narrative of movies. The ending however was taken over and totally rewritten by Cleese and Chapman.

8: "Full Frontal Nudity" December 7, 1969 (8) (November 23, 1969):

"Army Sketch", "Protection Racket" / "Vox pops" / "Art Critic" ("the place of the nude in my bed") / "Buying a Bed" / "Silly" / "Hermits" / "Dead Parrot" / "The Flasher" / "Hell's Grannies".

"Army Sketch", written by the combination of John Cleese and Michael Palin, features the notorious Vercotti brothers, Dino and Luigi. Dino seems to have disappeared after this episode although Luigi went on to have a full and rich life in other sketches. Strangely, considering its later infamy, "Dead Parrot" is fairly sedate here, with a confusion over whether or not the shop is in Ipswitch or Bolton taking center stage.

9: "The Ant: An Introduction" December 14, 1969 (10) December 7, 1969):

"Llama" / "A Man With a Tape Recorder up his Nose" / "Kilimanjaro Expedition" (double vision mountaineers) / "A Man With a Tape Recorder up his Brother's Nose" / "The Barber", "Lumberjack Song" / Crooner Gumby / The Refreshment Room at Bletchley / * "Brian Islam and Brucie" / "Hunting Film" /" The Unwelcome Visitors".

"Hunting Film", about a group of upper-class twits who go hunting, is very reminiscent of the hunting scene Cleese and Chapman wrote for the Peter Sellers / Ringo Starr movie *The Magic Christian*. "Unwelcome Visitors" also incorporates several abandoned ideas Cleese and Chapman wrote for the movie, including one about a shy man who accidentally sits on the host's cat and kills it. But this is not a wholly original idea as Terry Southern, the author of the book *The Magic Christian,* had a similar scene in his first book, *Flash and Filigree.*

10: December 21, 1969 (9) (November 30, 1969):

Walk-on part in sketch / "Bank Robber in Lingerie Shop" / "Trail" / "Arthur Tree" / "Vocational Guidance Consular", "Chartered Accountant" / "The First Man to Jump the Channel" / "Tunneling from Godalming to Java" / "Pet Conversions" / "Librarian-Gorilla" / Letters to the Daily Mirror / "Strangers in the Night".

"Arthur Tree" is Idle's thinly-veiled tribute to David Frost. "Vocational Guidance Counselor" features Palin as Mr. Entrophy, a very close relative of Arthur Putey. Notice the many references in this episode to homosexuality.

"Pet Conversions" had an interesting origin. It was written by Cleese and Chapman as a response to a BBC request that the group supply them a sketch for a Christmas anthology show. The group didn't want any part of the show, and the BBC didn't want them in it either when they read this sketch. Its inclusion here is the result of desperation for material, says Chapman. Also notice Cleese's tongue-in-cheek reference back to the "Dead Parrot" sketch. The dialog between the two "women" at the end of "The First Man to Jump the Channel" sketch is a non-too-subtle dig at the way the Radio Times described their show; calling it "zany" and "madcap." It also features the second appearance of Luigi Vercotti as Ron Obvious's manager.

11: December 28,1969 (11) (December 14, 1969):
"Letter (lavatorial humor)" / * / "Interruptions" / "Agatha Christie Sketch" / "Football Discussed in Literary Terms" / "Undertakers" / "Interesting People" / "18th Century Social Legislation" / "Where was the Battle of Trafalger Fought?" / "Batley Townswomens Guild presents the Battle of Pearl Harbor" / "Undertakers".

This episode starts off with a whimper, about the Philharmonic Orchestra going to the bathroom, making a very bad joke about "movements" (bowel and musical) and it doesn't get much cheerier. Lots of pointless references to undertakers and pained dialog about "someone being murdered" in the "Agatha Christie Sketch". Sharp eyes will notice that Terry Jones' *Keith Maniac of Guatemala* is an early attempt at his more successful *Amazing Mystico*. All in all (in my opinion) a very dull episode.

12: January 4, 1970 (12) (December 21, 1969):
"Falling From Building" / * "Magician" / "Spectrum" / " Talking About Things" / "Visitors from Coventry" / "Mr. Hilter" / "The Minehead By-Election" / "Police Station (funny voices)" / "Upper-Class Twit of the Year" / "Parental Consent" / "Ministerial Broadcast (falling through the earth's crust)".

There is a debate about who wrote "The Minehead By-Election" sketch. Some contend that it's a Cleese / Idle sketch while Chapman believes it's mainly Cleese / Chapman with a little input from all the others. Notice that the neighbor asleep in the bed during the "Upper-Class Twit of the Year" sketch looks a lot like ex-Bonzo Neil Innes.

13: January 11, 1970 (13) (January 4, 1970):
"Intermissions" / "Restaurant (abuse)", "Cannibalism" / "Intermission", "Advertisements" / "Albatross" / "Policeman (come back to my place)" / "Me doctor" / "Historical Impersonations" / "Quiz Program on Wishes" / "Probe-around Looks at Crime", "Stonehenge" / "Mr. Attlila the Hun" / "Psychiatry" / "Silly Sketch" / "Operating Theatre (squatters in patients stomach)".

"Restaurant (abuse)" is a sketch very reminiscent of a typical John and Mary exchange so popular when Cleese and Jo Kendall performed together on the radio series *I'm Sorry I'll Read That Again.* It also features the first reference to there being "a dead Bishop in the lobby," a phrase to gain more popularity in a later episode. Luigi Vercotti makes his third appearance as the manager of the La Gondola Restaurant. "Policeman" is another sketch whose authorship is much in debate. Cleese claims that he and Palin made the whole thing up on the spot, while Chapman contends that not only did he write it, but he was fairly upset when Cleese pinched the part of the policeman. "Historical Impersonations" features Chapman as a mime (Marcel Marceau) who first mimes being hit on top of the head with a 16 ton weight – then is actually crushed by a 16-ton weight. Cleese, Chapman, and Idle hated mimes. Jones is quite a very good mime.

Graham Chapman
(Cleese behind him)
on Python's first
American P.R. tour.

THE BEST LINES
OF THE FIRST SERIES

Monty Python had the unique ability to make a line of dialog memorable after only one viewing. Or else the line would be planted deep in you subconscious, where it would explode sometime later when you least expected it, causing you immense embarrassment as you cracked-up by yourself on the subway. Great lines also serve as great ice-breakers. I once had the pleasure of standing back stage with guitarist Jeff Beck, who was quiet and reserved – until I started quoting Python dialog. It seems that he is a fan, and soon we were both bouncing off the walls, laughing as we recreated the whole of the "Penguin on Top of the TV" sketch, funny voices and all. Sketches, like films, are remembered by their classic lines. You may not remember the plot of *Casablanca*, but you remember Bogart saying "Play it again, Sam." Below are some of the best lines of the first series.

```
Chapman, a farmer, has his sheep nesting in the
trees like birds.  JONES asks him where they got
the idea that they were birds:


CHAPMAN:   From Harold. He's that sheep over there
           under the elm.  He's that most dangerous
           of animals - a clever sheep.
```

JONES asks "Why not just get rid of Harold?" to which CHAPMAN replies:

CHAPMAN: Because of the enormous commercial possibilities should he succeed.

JONES is a CITY GENT in a bar. IDLE's the NUDGE-NUDGE MAN.

IDLE: Is your wife a goer? Eh? Eh? Know what I mean? Nudge-nudge, nudge-nudge, say no more, know what I mean?

JONES: I beg your pardon?

IDLE: Your wife, does she "go?" Eh? Eh? Eh? Know what I mean? Nudge-nudge.

JONES: Look, are you insinuating something?

IDLE: Oh nonononononononononono yes.

JONES: Well?

IDLE: I mean, you're a man of the world aren't you? I mean you've been there, haven't you? I mean you've been around...

JONES: What do you mean?

IDLE: I mean, well, you've...done it. I mean, well, you know, you've slept... with a lady...

JONES: Yes?

IDLE: What's it like?

CLEESE is a police inspector. JONES is a candy make:

CLEESE: Next we have number 4: Crunchy Frog.
            Am I right in thinking there's a real
            frog in here?

JONES: Yes, a little one.

CLEESE: What sort of frog?

JONES: A dead frog.

CLEESE: Is it cooked?

JONES: No.

CLEESE: What, a raw frog? . . .Don't you even
            take the bones out?

JONES: If we took the bones out it wouldn't be
            crunchy, would it!?

CLEESE has just taken his dead parrot, a Norwegian
Blue, back to PALIN who runs a pet shop:

PALIN: He's not dead, he's pining for the
            fjords.

CLEESE: Pining for the fjords!? This parrot's
            not pining mate — he's passed on!

CLEESE is a bandit who's robbing IDLE, manager of a lingerie shop:

CLEESE: Good morning, I'm a bank robber. Please don't panic, just hand over all your money.

IDLE: This is a lingerie shop, sir.

CLEESE: Fine… fine… um, no large piles of money in safes?

IDLE: No sir.

CLEESE: No deposit accounts?

IDLE: No sir.

CLEESE: No piles of cash in easy to carry bags?

IDLE: Not at all sir.

CLEESE: Fine… fine… Just a pair of knickers then, please.

JONES is Ron Obvious, about to make the first broadjump across the English Channel. He explains to interviewer CLEESE why it's actually easier to jump a great big bloody expanse of water rather than dry land:

JONES: Well, my manager explained it to me. You see, if you're five miles out over the English Channel, with nothing but sea underneath you, there is a great impetus to stay in the air.

CLEESE visits PALIN who again runs a pet shop. CLEESE wants to buy a cat, but all PALIN has to sell is a terrier. CLEESE isn't too interested:

PALIN: Listen, tell you what, I'll file his back legs down a bit, take his snout off, stick a few wires through his cheeks and there you are, a lovely pussy cat.

CLEESE: Not a proper cat.

PALIN: What do you mean?

CLEESE: Well it wouldn't meow.

PALIN: (shrugging) Well, he'll howl a bit.

PALIN is Ken Shabby, a vagrant who wants to marry CHAPMAN'S daughter CONNIE BOOTH. CHAPMAN, who's rich, asks Ken about his background:

CHAPMAN: And what sort of job do you do?

PALIN: I clean out public lavatories.

CHAPMAN: Is there promotion involved?

PALIN: Oh yes! (he coughs) After five years they give you a brush! Sorry Squire I gobbed on your carpet.

CHAPMAN: And when do you expect to get married?

PALIN: Oh, right away sport, right away! You know, I haven't had it for weeks!

CLEESE, in a nurse's uniform, stands in a theatre selling an albatross. JONES is a customer:

JONES: What flavor is it?

CLEESE: It's a bird isn't it? It's a bloody sea bird, it isn't any bloody flavor!

JONES: Do you get wafers with it?

CLEESE: 'Course you don't get bloody wafers with it! Albatross!

JONES: Well how much is it?

CLEESE: Ninepence.

JONES: I'll have two, please.

CLEESE: (calling) Gannet on a stick!

PALIN visits CHAPMAN, a surgeon, to have folk musicians removed from his stomach. When CHAPMAN operates he discovers IDLE and CLEVELAND inside the stomach:

CHAPMAN: (to PALIN) Are they paying you any rent?

PALIN: Of course they're not paying me any rent!

IDLE: (to PALIN) It's not furnished, you fascist!

A German version of "The Funniest Joke In the World":

HITLER: My dog has no nose.

SOLDIER: How does he smell?

HITLER: Awful!

CLEESE is explaining to interviewer JONES how he became a mouse / man:

CLEESE: Well, I was about seventeen and some mates and me went to a party and, well, we had quite a lot to drink… and some fellows there started… handing… cheese around. Well, just out of curiosity I tried some. And that was that.

JONES: What else did "these fellows" do?

CLEESE: Well, some of them started… dressing up as mice a bit… and then when they'd got the costumes on they started…. Squeaking.

CLEESE, a barrister, upon being asked if his client (in a coffin) is dead:

CLEESE: No, he's not completely dead, m'lud, no. But he's not at all well.

CHAPMAN is a guest on the show *Interesting People* where PALIN is the host. CHAPMAN has brought along his cat, Tiddles, which he claims can fly across the studio and land in a bucket of water.

PALIN: (astonished) By herself?

CHAPMAN: No, I fling her.

PALIN rushes up to CLEESE, a policeman, to tell him that 15 pounds has been taken from his wallet:

CLEESE: Did you see anyone take it? Anyone hanging about?

PALIN: No, there was no one there at all, that's the trouble.

CLEESE: Well, there's not much we can do about that, sir.

PALIN: (after a long pause) Do you… do you want to come back to my place?

CLEESE: (after a moment) Yeah. Alright.

THE SECOND SERIES

"AND NOW FOR SOMETHING COMPLETELY DIFFERENT"

Carol Cleveland and
John Cleese (looking
like the organist
from Deep Purple) in
'The Atillia The Hun
Show' sketch. This
was a
Cleese/Chapman
sketch spoofing what
few insipid American
sitcoms they'd seen
at that time.

THE SECOND SERIES

Sept. 15, 1970 - Dec. 22, 1970

By 1970 the effects of the new regime were being felt at the BBC. Ideas were no longer coming from the bottom – mandates were being issued at the top. Prime Minister Wilson lost the general election to Edward Heath in 1970, and one of Heath's first actions was to keep Lord Hill on at the BBC. Meanwhile, Lord Hill was taking his own steps to strengthen his position at Broadcasting House and, although the changes were ebbing in slowly, they were coming nonetheless. It was almost as if Auntie Beeb had suddenly stumbled drunkenly to the floor – intoxicated on her nine-year creative tonic–and lapsed into sleep. It was soon to become a coma.

The first series of *Monty Python* had been judged a success and a second series was commissioned by the BBC, along with a budget increase to about $8000 per episode, and the promise of a fixed transmission time and better publicity. Rehearsals and recording for the second series began in June that year, and it was during this time that the team was visited on the set by the BBC's Managing Director of Television, Huw Weldon. He told them that he had arranged a meeting for them with Program Controller for BBC-1, Paul Fox, to discuss the show. (The group had been so vexed at the irregular transmission dates and lack of, or sometimes worthless, publicity for the first series that they had already drafted a letter to Fox in complaint.) Fox's good news soon disintegrated into disappointment. Yes, they would be given an earlier and regular transmission date, he told them, just after 10 o'clock on Tuesday nights. That was certainly late enough, but unfortunately this was the time when the outer regions left the BBC network to show local fare. Consequentially only London and the Northern Region saw the second series the first time around. Scotland saw it on a different night. Repeats at a better time were promised.

Actually the team was lucky to have had another series commissioned at all. The changes at the BBC were such that, by the time the first series had actually been transmitted, those Powers That Be at the BBC were less than enthusiastic about its content. They thought that they were going to get another *That Was The Week That Was*-type satirical show, not this silly stuff. (The BBC has, in fact, been looking for another *TW3*-type program ever since the original left the airwaves.) It was mainly due to the laudatory ravings of the television critics that the show survived a first series and that a second one was commissioned. Although the numbers weren't too bad either. Despite the Beeb's accidental (?) efforts to kill the show (the irregular transmission times and the lack of publicity), the group managed to raise their ratings from one and a half million to three million viewers. And once, when the show had been accidentally transmitted as early as 9:45 p.m., the viewing figures nudged the four and a half-million mark.

The popularity of the show was mystifying to the executives at the BBC, but they knew a good thing when they had one.

The only word of caution being given was to John Cleese at a party towards the end of the first series from David Attenborough, then Director of Programs for BBC-2: "Use shock sparingly." Cleese admits it was sound advice, but that they never paid any attention to it. The second series, considered the best by fans and most of the team, was visibly different from the first in several ways. First of all, the budget increase meant that the sets could look less tawdry and that they could venture out a bit more and go on location. (They eventually got as exotic as filming "The Cycling Tour" in Jersey, one of the Channel Islands.) But perhaps the greatest difference was that the second series was the first to really feature new material, written especially for Monty Python. The series certainly contained some wonderful comic inventions: "The Ministry of Silly Walks" appeared in the first show transmitted (they continued the practice of airing the programs in a different order than they were recorded), followed by "The Spanish Inquisition", "The Semaphore Version of Wuthering Heights", "Spam", "The Piranha Brothers", and a host of other delightful absurdities. The team was at a creative peak, extremely confident and relaxed, and this showed in their work. So did their pre-occupation with program planners and other BBC officials, for they often used the show as a soapbox in which to vent their anger at these people, often using them (by name) as the butt of their jokes.

The Python style really began to come on strong during this series and, while they still clung desperately to a punch line if one was offered, the linking was better. They were successfully creating their own little world, with its own little rules, and one where the basic attitude was "piss off if you can't take a joke." Perhaps they should have listened a little closer to the friendly warnings of David Attenborough, for Mrs. Mary Whitehouse (who had no intention of pissing off) was beginning to take great exception to the series and to one item in particular, a sketch that appeared in the last show of the series, the aforementioned "Undertaker's" sketch. This sketch (as did the whole series) had a definite giddy "stick-that-in-your-pipe-and-smoke-it" feel to it; it was almost as if the team were determined to see exactly how much they could get away with. The niceties of the first series, the politeness with each other, had worn off and the basic idiosyncrasies of each individual member were beginning to seep through.

Cleese and Chapman, the writers of the notorious "Undertaker's" sketch, recall the morning that they wrote it as being one of the funniest of their lives; but that their laughter was more out of guilt than anything else. "It was the sheer awfulness of the idea that made it funny," says Chapman. Others did not agree. Paul Fox is quoted as saying that the program was continually going over the edge of what was acceptable, and he didn't really appreciate the group's treatment of the national anthem in the episode either. Cleese and Chapman knew the risks, as did the rest of the team, but their initial exuberance for the sketch nullified any concern. Still, director Ian MacNaughton was less sure of his ground, and so he followed the BBC practice of "referring it up" to Head of Comedy, Michael Mills. (MacNaughton had the most to lose, for at that time a producer was directly responsible for what went out under his name.) Mills read the script and decided that it would be all right for inclusion – so long as the audience was allowed to show their disgust by rushing the stage. (Hardly a realistic response.)

The look of fear that can be seen in the eyes of the group on the night of transmission can be attributed not to the audience's cat-calls, but rather to their fear that the audience won't react properly and rush the stage, thus negating the piece's inclusion in the program. What a Pythonic situation to be in! The other executives at the BBC were not as open-minded about the sketch as had been Michael Mills, and in the minutes of a meeting about the episode on the following day they bemoaned the group's current "death wish" and were also quite vexed that the sketch had been repeated later that evening on a BBC-2 discussion show called *Late Night Line-Up*. The went on to discuss how much they had enjoyed a program called *International Golf: The Best 18*.

But, for the most part, the second series was a happy time for the group. And a busy one. In addition to writing and performing in all 13 episodes of *Monty Python*, Graham Chapman also found the time to write scripts for *No That's Me Over Here*, a situation comedy starring Ronnie (*The Two Ronnies*) Corbett, and *11 Doctor In The House's*. Cleese became Rector of St. Andrew's

University. Gilliam did some freelance animation, while Idle edited the first of many Python books, *Monty Python's Big Red Book*. Python virtually invented the book-of-the-series market, and their legendary books (today almost unobtainable) were one of the first ways in which they broke away from the constraints of the BBC and assumed complete control over their work. *The Big Red Book* (in a decidedly blue jacket) featured a considerable amount of recycled television material, although it was recast in such a way as to parody print, with a few new ideas written especially for it by Idle and the group. Oddly, the rest of the team (especially Terry Gilliam) showed initial resistance to the idea. Gilliam (who'd had his fill of paste-up work on *Help!*) was not keen to be involved in the design, so Idle (the most literary of the group) hired an outside designer named Derek Birdsall to shoulder the project. Together they locked themselves in a little room at Methuen (the publishing house) and reportedly did not emerge until they had manufactured a respectable dummy of the book. (They also had reportedly broken into Gilliam's studio to nick the odd piece of artwork.) But, it being Python, there had to be trouble on the horizon. Strangely enough it came from a firm called the Wright Ukulele Tutor. The team had used the trademark of the Wright Ukulele Tutor on a piece of sheet music advertising their Song for Europe, "Bing Tiddle Tiddle Bong", but not as satire, rather to lend "authenticity" to the song. The company cried breach of copyright and threatened an injunction against the book just as it was starting to become a runaway best seller. Taking matters into their own hands, they altered the offending piece of sheet music after the first 75,000 copies had been printed, and the Wright Ukulele Tutor firm relinquished their grasp. Still not out of the woods, their parody of the W.H. Smith-Doubleday Literary Guild (which offered a free vat of dung and a dead Indian with book orders) negated their inclusion as a book club edition.

In October 1970 they all gathered together at a deserted milk depot in Totteridge to lens their first film, *And Now For Something Completely Different*. It was not a move, or a movie, that they all agreed was necessary. At this point in their careers there seemed little chance that the series would ever be shown in America. This was mainly due to their refusal to allow the shows to be edited, either on the grounds of censorship or for the insertion of commercials – yet they wanted desperately to break into the vast American market. So in August 1970 they had formed Python Productions Ltd. At the urging of Victor Lownes, who managed the London Playboy Club.

It was a move designed to give them more artistic control over their work. Lownes' first suggestion was to do a feature film of their television material and aim it at the always-fertile U.S. college crowd. Discussion, pro and con, over such a move ricocheted around the Python camp. What, some asked, was the possible benefit of a virtual rehash of old material – some of which had just been rehashed already in the *Big Red Book*? But when it was pointed out that the material wasn't old to the Americans and that, after all, a film is a film, a step up from television, the doubting Pythons agreed to do it.

Directed by Ian MacNaughton, *And Now For Something Completely Different* was filmed from October to November 1970, and released a year later. Few of its sketches benefit by being blown up to 35mm, and apart for a few special bits concocted especially for the film, it is virtually nothing more than a "best of Python" done for the silver screen. But the group had no real illusions of it ever being otherwise. The only real disagreements over it concerned the appearance of Palin's character Ken Shabby and the size of Lownes' credit. Ken Shabby lost the day, and was excised from the film, while Lownes won the day by hiring an outside animator to redesign his credit after Gilliam walked away from the battle in disgust. Ironically, the *raison d'etre* of the project fell apart: the film did virtually nothing in America, while in Britain, where the sketches were already old news, it did bang-up business, easily recouping Lownes' modest investment of about $150,000. The film had been a noble failure in a lot of ways, but the groundwork for the team's future independence had been laid.

The Pythons were beginning to see their intrinsic value as a team – which was a bit of a pity, for just as unity of purpose was starting to blossom, John Cleese began making noises about wanting to abandon ship.

John Marwood Cleese is a man who is bored very easily. He is a perfectionist who believes that if something is to be done then it should be done right – and that it should be done once. He has often been quoted as saying that he'd only wanted to do the occasional television program with the others, he didn't want to marry them! Where the others in the group were wanting to hang on and make good while the sun shined, Cleese was complaining that Python was taking up too much of his time (10 months a year by his calculations). He also moaned that they were beginning to repeat themselves; exploring the cruel and unusual in a desperate search for humor (odd comments from the co-author of "The Undertakers Sketch"). Still, despite these comments, something deep within the Cleese psyche ("Probably the whiff of money," joked Chapman) made him stay on with the group, and he buried his feelings of dissatisfaction in shallow sand.

John rues the day he
performed this
sketch as he's been
asked to 'do the
funny walk' almost
every day since.

THE EPISODES

The episodes are listed in chronological order of original transmissions, with original transmission date, number in order of recording (in brackets) and date of recording (also in brackets). The transmission order of the first three series was different from the order in which they were recorded so that the best shows could be placed first and last in the series.

A few sketches were transferred to a different show after they were edited, and some shows have a subtitle. In most cases these subtitles were rejected names for the series, but not always. The series were recorded in two marathon sessions, which accounts for the dual dates under series headings. Compiling a running order for *Monty Python's Flying Circus* has been compared to trying to make a set of blueprints for a surrealist painting; the shows hardly ever have sketches that begin and end in the traditional sense. Consequently the details below are merely indications as to the content of a sketch.

Principal animation links are indicated by an asterisk (*), and are occasionally given titles, but, as they are usually more surreal than the sketches, even the team themselves soon gave up any hope of describing them in their scripts and just indicated where they should go.

The shows were written and performed entirely by Graham Chapman, John Cleese (except most of the fourth series), Eric Idle, Terry Jones, and Michael Palin. Special appearances are made by Carol Cleveland, Connie Booth, and Mrs. Idle (Eric's first wife). Animations and occasional appearances are by Terry Gilliam.

Interesting trivia surrounding the writing, performing, or reception of a sketch is detailed in brackets {} at the end of each episode.

John Cleese and Michael Palin in 'The Fish-Slapping Dance', cited by most members as one of their all-time favorite sketches.

SECOND SERIES

September 15, 1970 – September 29, 1970
October 20, 1970 – December 22, 1970

1: September 15, 1970 (4) (July 9, 1970):
"Face the Press" / "Gas cooker sketch" / * / "Tobacconists", "Prostitute Advert" / "The Ministry of Silly Walks" / "Ethel The Frog": The story of Dinsdale Pirhana.

"The Ministry of Silly Walks" was written by Palin and Jones, yet was originally an idea of Cleese and Chapman. It seems that they had the idea a little too close to lunchtime and so, rather than risk missing lunch, they called up Mike and Terry and told them the idea, suggesting that they, in fact, write it.

2: September 22, 1970 (3) (July 2, 1970):
"Man-powered flight" / "Trouble at t'mill" / "Spanish Inquisition" / "Film line" / "Joke salesman" / "Missing punch line" / * / "Tax on 'thingy'" / "Vox pops" / "Photos of Uncle Ted, Spanish Inquisition" / * "I confess" / "The semaphore version of Wuthering Heights" / "Julius Caesar on an Aldis lamp" / Court scene (charades) / "Spanish Inquisition".

3: September 29, 1970 (5) (July 16, 1970).
"A Bishop Rehearsing" / "Flying Lessons" / "Plane Hijack to Luton" / "The Poet McTeagle" / * / " Milkman-Psychiatrists" / "Complaints" / "Déjà vu".

4: October 20, 1970 (9) (September 18, 1970):
*"Butterfly" / "Architect Sketch" / "How to Give up Being a Mason" / "Motor Insurance Sketch" / "The Bishop" / "Living on the Pavement", "Poet in the Bath" / "A Choice of Viewing" / Poets / * / Chemist Sketch" / Apology / "Words Not to be Used Again" / "After Shave" / "Vox Pops" / "Police Constable Pan Am"

Gilliam's cartoon, "Butterfly", is enshrined in London's Victoria and Albert Museum as a prime example of 1960s Pop culture.

5: October 27, 1970 (7) (September 10,1970):
"Live from the Grill-O-Mat Snack Bar in Paignton" / "Blackmail" / "National Society For Putting Things On Top of Other Thing"s / "P.O.W. escape,"* / "Current Affairs" / * / Accidents Sketch / "Seven Brides for Seven Brothers" / * "Piggy Bank Hunting" / "The Man Whose First Answer is Always a Rude One" / "Tea or Coffee link" / "Boxer documentary" / Closing live from on top of bus.

Gilliam's "Piggy Bank Hunting" features Teddy and Neddy, two characters very similar to Teddy and Freddy which Graeme Garden and Tim Brooke-Taylor featured on a program called *Broaden Your Mind*, and which may in fact be voiced here by them.

6: November 3, 1970 (8) (September 10,1970):
"It's A Living" / "The Time on BBC-1", / "Opening Titles" / "School Prize Giving" / "Mr. Dibley's Films of 'If' and 'Rear Window'" / "Foreign Secretary" / "Dung", "Dead Indian", "Police prizes" / * / "Interview with Timmy Williams" (David Frost skit) / "Mr. Raymond Luxury-Yacht" / * / "Registry Office" / * "The Spot" / "Election Night Special (Silly Party)".

"Mr. Dibley's Films…" is notable because Dibley was, of course, on of the rejected names for Monty Python. "Foreign Secretary" features an appearance by Python film editor Ray Millichope. Gilliam's "The Spot" was the victim of BBC censorship. Originally the Prince died of cancer, but it was later changed to gangrene. Ironically, Graham Chapman (who died of cancer) was the most vocal about this, saying it's best to talk about things like cancer rather than deny their existence.

7: November 10, 1970 (11) October 2, 1970):
"The Attila The Hun Show" / "Attlia The Nun" / "Secretary of State" (striptease) / "Vox pops on politicians" / "Rat catcher" / "Sheep in the wainscoting" / "Killer sheep" / * "Basil the killer sheep" / "The news for parrots" / "The news for gibbons" / "Today in Parliament" / "The news for wombats" / * "Attila The Bun" / "The idiot in society" / "The test match" / "Cricket played by furniture" / "The Epsom Furniture Race" / "Take Your Pick".

"Take Your Pick" was replaced by "The Agatha Christie Sketch" from show 11 when the show was repeated on August 23, 1971, due to the death of Michael Miles, a game show host. "The Attila The Hun Show" was written by Cleese and Chapman as an attack on the few American sitcoms they'd seen, such as *The Donna Reed Show*. There's a lot of striptease in Python ("Secretary of State"), usually male, and its logical precedent is the striptease scene Cleese and Chapman wrote for *The Magic Christian* where an actor strips while doing *Hamlet*. In "Take Your Pick" Jones plays Mrs. Scum, later Mrs. S.c.u.m. in the "Mr. Neutron" episode in series four. Cleese also mentions the philosopher Henri Bergson in this sketch. He is a favorite of Cleese's and is mentioned several times in various episodes.

8: November 17, 1970 (12) October 9, 1970):
"Trailer" / * / "Archeology Today" / "Arthur Belling" (the silly vicar) / "Leapy Lee" / "Registrar" (wife change) / "Silly Doctor Sketch" (immediately abandoned) / * "Book Advert" / "Mr. And Mrs. Git" / "Mosquito

Hunters" / "Poofy Judges" / "Mrs. Thing and Mrs. Entity" / "Beethoven and His Mynah Bird" / "Shakespeare" / "Michelangelo" / "Colin Mozart" (the rat catcher) / "Judges".

The roots of the "Mosquito Hunters" can also be found in *The Magic Christian*. The idea of attacking small creatures with missiles and bazookas is very much like the scene where Peter Sellers and Ringo Starr hunted pigeons using heavy artillery. The idea of Beethoven composing other tunes while trying to write "The Fifth Symphony" was revived years later on *Saturday Night Live* with John Belushi playing Beethoven and composing "My Girl" – but never "The Fifth Symphony."

9: November 24, 1970 (10) (September 15, 1970):
"How to Recognize Different Parts of the Body" / "Bruces" / "More Parts of the Body" / "Norman St. John Polevaulter (the man who contradicts people)" / "More Parts of the Body" / "Mr. Luxury-Yacht" / "Cosmetic Surgery" / "Square Bashing" ("squad – camp it – up!") * "Killer Cars" / "Cut Price Airline" / "Batley Townswomen's Guild Presents the First Heart Transplant" / "The First Underwater Production of 'Measure For Measure'" / "More Parts of the Body" / "The Death of Mary Queen of Scots" / "Penguin on the TV" / "More Parts of the Body" / "There's Been a Murder" / Europolice Song Contest, Song: "Bing Tiddle Tiddle Bong."

The joke about how "New Bruce can teach about socialism – as long as he makes it clear that it's wrong" in "Bruces", is a dig at Terry Jones who is an avid socialist in real life. On the group's LP, *Matching Tie and Handkerchief,* this same sketch ends with the "Drunken Philosopher's Song" – but here it just leads back into how to recognize more body parts. The idea behind "The Death of Mary Queen of Scots", written by Palin and Jones, was originally suggested by David Sherlock. He thought it would really be funny to have a TV show that consisted of people sitting around listening to the radio. If you watch the faces of Cleese and Chapman during this sketch you can see that they appear to be on the verge of laughing. They are. Chapman has said that they had to do several takes of this sketch as they kept breaking themselves up during filming. There's a funny moment during "There's Been a Murder" where Palin (playing the police inspector) gives Chapman a bit of the same medicine that he dished out to Terry Jones in episode three, during the sketch where Jones wanted to learn how to fly "an aero-plane." Also, at the tail end of this sketch we can see that Idle is wearing a lampshade on his head for no apparent reason, and that Cleese is looking very bored during Terry Jones' song.

10: December 1, 1970 (2) (July 2, 1970):
"French Subtitled Film" / "Shooting 'Scott of the Antarctic'" / "Scott of the Sahara" / Opening Titles / * "Dancing Teeth" / "Fish License" / "Council" / "Football Match" / "Long John Silver Impersonators Versus the Bournemouth Gynecologists".

The director Cleese impersonates in "Scott of the Antarctic", James McCretin, is not, as widely believed, a take on Python director Ian MacNaughton. It is instead a take on *Magic Christian* director James McGrath. The role of Miss Evans is played with much comic intuition by Carol Cleveland. She says that it was one of the few starring roles she got in the series and quite enjoyed the chance to act. Sharp eyes will notice that Eric Praline (Cleese) walks up to a window belonging to a Mr. Balfour in "Fish License". This name, and the man behind the window, is Python cameraman James Balfour. Palin stands behind the nameplate of a Mr. Last, who was production assistant Roger Last. The Cleese / Idle song, "Eric The Half A Bee" was originally supposed to be included in the "Fish License" sketch, but was excised.

11: December 8, 1970 (6) (July 23, 1970):
"Conquistador Coffee Campaign" / "Repeating Groove" / Opening titles / "Ramsay MacDonald Striptease" / * "Ad for American Defense and Krelm Toothpaste" / "Agatha Christie Sketch" (railway timetables) / "Mr. Nevile Shunt" (the author), "Review of Timetable" / "Film Director with

Large Front Teeth" / "City Gents Vox Pops" / "Crackpot Religions Ltd." / * / "How Not to be Seen" / "Man who Crossed the Atlantic on a Tricycle" / "Goalkeeper in a File Cabinet" / * / "Yummy Yummy" / Speeded-up repeat of entire show.

There's a running theme in this episode of things being stuck. And, again, we have a striptease. "Vox Pops" features Idle doing a rather good impersonation of John Lennon. He has now done both Lennon and McCartney (Dirk McQuickly of the Rutles.)

12: December 15 1970 (1) (June 25, 1970):

"The Black Eagle" / "Dirty Hungaraian Phrasebook" / "Court" / * / "World Forum" / "Communist Quiz" / "Ypres 1914" / "Art gallery" (the "man from the Hay Wain") / "Ypres 1914" / "Hospital for Over-actors" / "Flower Arrangement" / "Vikings in Transport Café" / "Spam".

"Ypres 1914" caused discomfort at Television Center. It seems that BBC officials didn't like the idea of the team sending up World War One. Country music fans might be interested to notice that the title of the Bellamy Brother's hit, "If I Said You Had A Beautiful Body Would You Hold It Against Me?" is first uttered here by John Cleese, at the end of "Spam."

13: December 22, 1970 (13) October 16, 1970):

"The Queen Will be Watching" / Royal opening titles / "Coalminer's Historical Argument" / "A Man who Says Things in a Roundabout way, A Man who Speaks Only the End of Words, A Man who Speaks Only the Beginning of Words, A Man who Speaks Only the Middle of Words" / "Commercials" / "How to Feed a Goldfish" / "The Man who Collects Birdwatcher's Eggs" / * / "Insurance Sketch" / "The Queen is Now Watching" / "Hospital Ward Run by Sergeant Major" / "Mountaineer Sketch" / "Exploding Version of "The Blue Danube" / "The Naughtiest Girl In School" / "Mrs. Nesbitt's headache" / * / "Letters to the BBC" / "A

Man with a Stoat Through his Head" / "Still no Sign of Land" / "The Undertakers Sketch" / "The Queen is Watching Again" / End titles with "God Save the Queen."

After the "Coalminers" sketch, Palin introduces "The Toad Elevating Moment", which was another rejected title for the show. The guest on this show, "A Man who Speaks in a Roundabout Manner" (Jones), is based on David Sherlock. He used to catch all sorts of flack from the others for speaking very indirectly. "The Exploding Version of The Blue Danube" was done live in one take using real explosives. "The Man who Collects Birdwatcher's Eggs" is based on Terry Jones' brother, Nigel, who delighted in mundane activities.

An example of the wrong way to handle customer complaints. Terry Jones, John Cleese (in the hat) and Graham Chapman from the 'Dirty Fork Sketch'

THE BEST LINES OF SECOND SERIES

Chapman, in drag, is the Minister For Home Affairs being quizzed by Idle as to why the government has built only three of the promised 88 thousand-million-billion low-income homes over the last 15 years:

CHAPMAN: I'd like to answer that question, if I may, in two ways. Firstly in my normal voice, and then in a kind of silly high-pitched whine.

Chapman is Vince Snetterton-Lewis, a small-time operator who fell foul of Doug and Dinsdale Piranha:

CHAPMAN: Well, one day I was sitting at home, threatening the kids, and I look out through the hole in the wall and I saw this tank drive up and one of Dinsdale's boys gets out. He comes up all nice and friendly-like and says Dinsdale wants to have a talk with me. So, he chains me to the back of the tank and takes me for a scrape 'round to Dinsdale's place. And Dinsdale's there, in the conversation pit with Doug and Charles Paisley the Baby Crusher, and a couple of film producers and a man they called Kierkegaard who just sat there biting the heads off whippets.

Palin is Cardinal Ximinez, leader of the Spanish Inquisition, who's just surprised Cleveland and Chapman:

PALIN: Nobody expects the Spanish Inquisition! Our chief weapon is surprise. Surprise and fear. Fear and Surprise… our two weapons are fear and surprise. And a ruthless efficiency. Our three weapons are fear and surprise and ruthless efficiency and an almost fanatical devotion to the Pope. Our four…no…amongst our weapons…amongst our weaponry are such diverse elements as fear, surprise… I'll come in again.

"Lend Us A Quid 'Til The End Of The Week"
A poem by Ewen McTeagle:

Lend us a quid 'til the end of the week

If you could see your way

To lending me sixpence

I could at least buy a newspaper

That's not much to ask anyone

Palin is a doctor, underneath a kilt worn by Cleese:

PALIN: (to camera) Look, would you mind going
            away? I'm trying to examine this man.
            Uh… it's alright, I'm a doctor.
            Actually, I'm a gynecologist, but this
            is my lunch hour.

Cleese is an architect whose design for an apartment block includes rotating knives and blood troughs. He mainly designs slaughterhouses. Palin and Jones, the ones wanting the apartments built don't like his design:

CLEESE: Yes, well, that's just the sort of
            blinkered philistine pig-ignorance I've
            come to expect from you non-creative
            garbage. You sit there on your loath-
            some, spotty behinds squeezing black-
            heads, not giving a tinker's cuss about

the struggling artist. You excrement!
You lousy hypocritical whining toadies!
With your lousy color TVs and your Tony
Jacklin golf clubs and you bleedin'
Masonic handshakes... You wouldn't let me
join, would you? You blackballing bas-
tards! Well I wouldn't become a
Freemason now if you went down on your
lousy, stinking, purulent knees and
begged me!

Palin is a BBC Voice-Over Announcer:

PALIN: Well, it's five past nine and nearly
time for six past nine. On BBC-2 it
will shortly be six and a half minutes
past nine. Later on this evening it
will be ten o'clock, and at ten-thirty
we'll be going over to BBC-2 in time
for ten thirty-three. And don't forget
tomorrow when it'll be nine-twenty.
Those of you who missed eight forty-
five of Friday will be able to see it
again this Friday at a quarter to nine.
Now here's a time change, it's six and a
half minutes to the big green thing.

Palin goes to answer the door. Outside is Cleese
with his free tub of dung:

PALIN: I didn't order any dung!

CLEESE: Yes you did, sir. You ordered it

through the Book of The Month Club.
With every third book ordered you get a
free tub of dung.

Idle and Chapman are hunting mosquitoes, using
heavy artillery:

CHAPMAN: I've been a hunter all my life. I love
           animals, that's why I like to kill 'em.

IDLE: The mosquito's a clever little bastard,
           you can track him for days and days
           until you get to know him like a
           friend. It's a game of wits. You hate
           him, then you respect him… then you
           kill him.

The whole group are members of an Australian philosophy department, welcoming new teacher Jones to
their midst:

CLEESE: Right then gentlemen, I'll just remind
           you of the facility rules. Rule one, no
           poofters. Rule two, no member of the
           facility is to maltreat the abo's in
           anyway whatsoever…if there's anyone
           watching. Rule three, no poofters. Rule
           four, I don't want to catch anyone not
           drinking in their room after lights-
           out. Rule five, no poofters. Rule six,
           there is no rule six! Rule seven, no
           poofters!

Cleese and Chapman are Pepperpots who have just discovered a penguin on top of their TV:

CLEESE: Funny that penguin being there, isn't it? What's it doing there?

CHAPMAN: Standing.

CLEESE: I can see that!

CHAPMAN: If it lays an egg, it will fall down the back of the television set.

CLEESE: We'll have to watch that. Unless it's a male.

CHAPMAN: Ooh, I never thought of that.

CLEESE: (after peering at the penguin closely) Yes... it looks fairly butch.

Cleese, as Eric Praline, is telling postal worker Palin about the license he had to buy for his pet cat Eric. Palin says that he doesn't need a cat license:

CLEESE: You bleedin' well do, and I got one! You're not catching me out there!

He hands the license to Palin who says that it's a dog license with the word dog crossed out and the word cat written in crayon:

CLEESE: The man didn't have the proper form.

Cleese has come to visit Chapman, who is an under-taker, because his mother has just died:

CHAPMAN: There are three things we can do with you mother: we could burn her, bury her , or dump her.

CLEESE: (shocked) Dump her!?

CHAPMAN: Dump her in the Thames.

CLEESE: What?!

CHAPMAN: Oh, did you like her?

CLEESE: Why, yes.

CHAPMAN: Oh, we won't dump her then.

They eventually decide to eat her. But Cleese is having second thoughts.

CHAPMAN: Look, tell you what… we'll eat her, and if you feel a bit guilty about it afterwards… we can dig a grave and you can throw up into it.

The boys give a lecture on the correct way to do slapstick. From left: Michael Palin, Terry 'Custard Pie' Jones, Terry Gilliam and Graham Chapman.

THE THIRD SERIES

"NOBODY EXPECTS THE SPANISH INQUISITION"

Terry Jones gets an
earful. From left:
Terry Jones, Terry
Gilliam and Graham
Chapman

THE THIRD SERIES

Oct. 19, 1972 - Jan. 18, 1973

The Pythons spent the majority of 1971 on film. No new series had been offered by the BBC so they concentrated their efforts instead on those projects that would benefit them more personally. Aside from *And Now For Something Completely Different* (which was shaping up as a success in Britain), the team also made some advertising films for industry. These "industrials" were not intended for viewing by the general public, rather by salesmen, so that they could learn more about a product or service. Many ideas that appeared later in the third series had their origins in these films (the sketch "Whicker's World" is one such example).

1971 was also the year that they recorded their first LP for their own Python Productions, entitled *Another Monty Python Record* (Charisma CAS 1049). This LP was streets ahead of their first one *Monty Python's Flying Circus* (BBC Records REB 73m) in that this time around the group had complete artistic control. The first LP (which they didn't want to make) had been recorded at the urging of the BBC, and was a compilation of the best first series sketches. After their initial reticence, the group decided to go ahead and make the LP (and even went to a lot of bother working out complicated stereo effects and sound cues) only to arrive at the BBC Paris Studio and discover that, not only would they be recorded in mono, but that, for the most part, it would be done live in front of an uninvited studio audience. After much painstaking work the group was able to produce a rough version of a radio show. This LP, like their first film, is not viewed with much misty-eyed nostalgia by the group.

On the personal front, 1971 was the year that Graham Chapman became legal guardian to John Tomiczek (who later served as his personal manager until his death in 1991. The complete story of Graham and John Tomiczek can be found in Chapman's book, *A Liar's Autobiography*). Also in 1971, John Cleese and Connie Booth had a daughter, Cynthia (who was later to appear with dad in Cleese's 1988 film *A Fish Called Wanda* as, what else, his daughter). In April of that year the BBC submitted as their entry in the Montreaux Television Festival a compilation of Python shows, and to everyone's amazement it snagged the Silver Rose award. (Although the BBC Handbook for 1972 merely lists the prize alongside various other accolades the series had won, making no excessive mention of it.) As the critical ravings for the first series had helped secure a second one, this award opened the door for the BBC to commission a third. Everyone was pleased, with the possible exception of John Cleese. His reservations for continuing the series cropped up again, and this time he was not so easily mollified. He grudgingly agreed to do seven shows, but says that he was "somehow pressured" into doing all 13. Cleese's twitchiness was viewed with some disdain by the rest of the team, in fact, tensions inside the Python camp were mounting. They'd been working nearly non-stop for the last two years, and were virtually living inside one another's pockets.

Chapman: "You felt as if you had to ring the others up and ask if it was okay to have a bath." Differences were not being settled as amicably as before. The infamous Cleese / Jones confrontations in the writing-meetings sometimes took on the air of a cat fight; the more tweaking and goading Cleese became, the more adamant and single-minded Jones became until he would ultimately explode into a high-pitched Welsh whine (much to Cleese's amusement). Again, Terry Jones chooses to disagree.

Jones: "I sometimes think, when I read what the others thought about Python, that it's a bit as if they've read it in a book. I mean, all that stuff about me and John being opposites. But then, on the other hand, maybe it's in books about Python because we'd said it in the first place."

At the urging of director Ian MacNaughton the team flew to Germany to film a special (titled *Monty Python's Fliegende Zirkus*) for Bavarian Television. (Why Germany? Again, Ian MacNaughton had a girlfriend there.) Upon arrival at the studio they discovered to their horror that they were expected to do their lines *in German*. They managed to do this phonetically, but, even so, the language presented some problems. It was quickly discovered that German really wasn't a language structured for their jokes, it's phrasing being somewhat cumbersome. As an example, in the "Stake Your Claim" sketch, Chapman plays a woman named Mrs. Mund (Mrs. Mouth) whose claim to fame was that she could "burrow through an elephant." Now, this is an awfully silly line in normal enough English, but the literal translation of it in German became "I, through an elephant, do burrow." It doesn't exactly carry the same comic payload… Several other never before seen sketches include a delightful one about a couple who visit a Bavarain restaurant and order what German waiter Cleese says are "authentic Bavarian dishes." These include dousing the couple with a bucket of pig urine, verbal, physical, and other unmentionable abuses soon follow. This special, never transmitted outside Germany (where it was seen once) was later purchased by the group (along with a second one they did in 1972) with the money they won in a later lawsuit judgement against ABC-TV. These films now sit gathering dust on a shelf, perhaps forever, as the group can't decide what to do with them. (NOTE: They *did* receive a brief showing on Showtime in 1990, as part of a 20th anniversary salute to Python. The Comedy Central comedy channel also showed them both in January 1995. Both videos were released in fall 1998 by Guerilla Films: www.guerilla.u-net.com)

1971 was also a difficult year for the BBC. Tensions were mounting in Northern Ireland and, against the wishes of Home Secretary Reginald Maudling, the Beeb elected to air *The Question of Ulster: An Enquiry into the Future*, a TV film that took a hard (and unpopular) look at the problems. Lord Hill was playing both ends against the middle; while on the one hand he resisted Mary Whitehouse's demand for the creation of a Broadcasting Council, he then turned around and set-up his own watchdog organization called The Advisory Group on the Social Effects of Television. Hill's plan was to fend-off outside pressures while asking his own executives to look into "matters of taste and sex." What he wanted was self-censorship. These discussions were to continue well into 1972, just in time for the decisions reached by the committee to affect the third series of *Monty Python*.

Rehearsals and recordings for the third series began in December of 1971, and lasted until May 1972. The entire third series was recorded before the first episode (the fifth one to be recorded) was transmitted on October 19th, 1972. On the final day of recording, May 25th, 1972, the team were surprised to have visitors on the set: Bill Cotton, The Head of Light Entertainment; and Duncan Wood, the Head of Comedy. The Pythons heard later, in the BBC Club, that the two men had been "none too pleased" with the last two episodes that the group had recorded. Not pleased at all. The Pythons thought that most interesting, but hardly Earth-shattering, news and immediately left again for Germany where they were set to do another special for Bavarian Television (this time in English, much to their relief).

Early in 1972 Lord Hill received a delegation from the Nationwide Festival of Light, an off-shoot of, though not directly connected with Mary Whitehouse's National Vala. The group later presented Hill with a paper which outlined their concerns that creative artists were continually hiding behind "artistic freedoms" in order to go to lengths which were indefensible for the BBC. Lord Hill was inclined to agree. (In his defense it must be noted that Hill was trying to please everyone, and while he did press for cuts, he attempted to allow an atmosphere to develop where the producers and artist themselves did the cuts. The problem was, the Pythons didn't want any censorship. Quite rightly.)

While in Germany, MacNaughton received a letter from Cotton and Wood which further outlined their problems with the last two episodes of Monty Python. This letter became known as the "32 Points of Worry", for in it they listed 32 causes for concern about these shows. While no copy of this letter appears to have survived, the majority of these concerns concentrated on the simulated rape scene in "The Dirty Vicar Sketch", the word "masturbating" in the "All-England Summarize Proust" sketch, most of a sketch about Oscar Wilde insulting the Prince of Wales and a sketch (since deleted on the videotape) about a bar where patrons can order disgusting drinks like Mallard Fizz with a "twist of lemming." They also wanted the team to cannibalize shows 12 and 13 and make one, acceptable, show out of it. Needless to say, the Pythons refused.

MacNaughton tried to deflect the cuts at first, and was answered with a much sterner letter demanding them. MacNaughton was in an unenviable position. He was torn between his loyalty to the group and his duty as an employee of the BBC to carry out their demands. While he procrastinated, a third letter arrived from Cotton and Wood offering up other bits for the chopping block. The group was stunned. The ugly fist of censorship, which had always threatened but never appeared, was now knocking on the door. At the Pythons request, MacNaughton arranged a meeting between them and Duncan Wood. On October 27, 1972, all six Pythons and MacNaughton crowded into Wood's tiny office at the BBC to discuss "what can and can not be said on a comedy series." Although Terry Jones made a spirited defense for masturbation ("I masturbate, you masturbate..."), the group's main objection was to the amount of cuts on a show airing well after 10 o'clock at night. Wood stammered and made vague references to "pressures from the outside" and "heat from above." The group took this to mean that Paul Fox, Controller of BBC-1, was the culprit. To back up the claim they noticed that one of the cuts being demanded was a cartoon of Fox which depicted him as a good fairy who kisses a man, thus turning him into a frog. But they were wrong; Fox hadn't even seen the offending program.

A viewing was arranged (with the unusual stipulation that MacNaughton not be allowed to sit in), and Fox decided that only three minor cuts were needed. It was already too late to save the "All-England Summarize Proust" sketch as the word "masturbating" had already been edited out (actually it's said so softly, and the audience reaction is so loud that you can hardly hear it anyway). With that settled, the Pythons returned to Germany to finish their special.

The second German special should be of interest to Python fans as it includes several sketches never before seen in America. Among the highlights is the infamous "Philosopher's Football" sketch in which two teams made up entirely of famous philosophers merely wander around thinking, profoundly ignoring the football; a running gag about grizzled old prospectors who pan, not for gold, but for rabbits; a funny (if predictable) sketch about confusion in a hearing–aid and contact lens shop (it originally aired on *At Last The 1948 Show*); and a fairly long Cleese / Booth fairy tale called "Happy Valley, Or, The Princess With The Wooden Teeth". (This sketch can be found in written form in *The Brand New Monty Python Book* and in recorded form on their *Monty Python's Previous Record* LP.) this special was later transmitted by the BBC in October 1973 as *Schnapps With Everything*. The German trip sticks out in Chapman's mind for quite a different reason: it was one of the few times he ever saw John Cleese let go and have a good time. "He was jolly for an entire day," says Chapman. "He just laughed and giggled and was friendly to people…he finds that very difficult, normally." Of course, it was Oktoberfest.

Much has been made of the Pythons' preoccupation with philosophers (especially in the third series) and, in fact, Johnathan (*Beyond The Fringe*) Miller has even singled out the "All-England Summarize Proust" sketch as being an example of the intellectualism of Monty Python. In reality it is a clever smoke screen. Make no mistake, the group isn't a load of dumb bunnies, but (as has been admitted) their knowledge of famous philosophers is merely a varnish. They may know enough to maybe work out the name in a crossword, but they don't necessarily have a deep understanding of the man and his work. Nor did they have to in order for it to be funny. Perhaps as Cleese's Dennis Moore would say, "This is a comedy series, not a primer in modern philosophy!"

The group also found time that year to record another LP (*Monty Python's Previous Record* Charisma CAS 1063), compile another book of the series (*The Brand New Monty Python Bok*) and prepare to embark on a stage tour of Canada and the United Kingdom. *The Bok* was again edited by Eric Idle, designed this time by Kate Hepburn. This time around, Methuen (the publishing house) decided to avoid the problems of the first book at the start and so sent rough proofs of the book to the firm's attorney, Michael Rubinstein, as it progressed. For the most part Rubinstein found it clean of any possible litigation, but the printers were not so sure. They sought their own legal advice form the firm of Chapman and Company and, to their dismay, they discovered a whole new set of litigious possibilities. Feeling that delay was the better part of prudence, the printers balked. This was a move that put Methuen at a disadvantage, for they were aiming at the lucrative Christmas market and delay in printing could mean that they would miss their prime buying season for the Bok. In desperation they attempted to contact Idle, to see what legal advice the group had received, but he had already left to join the others in Canada. Mr. Roydon Thomas, a Python attorney, was available for comment, though, and he sent Methuen a 10 page letter outlining the "Python Philosophy". On hindsight, the group's solicitos, Denton Hall, sent a two page letter to Michael Rubinstein offering "Six Points of Concern" about the Bok. Among these concerns was the cover page of "16" magazine, the possibility of there being a real life Col. Sir Harry McWhirter M.C.C., and the article entitled "How to become a Segas employee". This last item worried them as they had no idea what it was supposed to mean. Methuen and Python Productions Ltd. Decided to go ahead and indemnify the printers against libel. Methuen did this immediately, anxious as they were to get the book out in time for Christmas. But in their haste they forgot about the top right-hand corner of page 65. It was an excerpt from Idle's "Spanish Holiday" sketch, and was a matter for possible prosecution for obscenity, not libel, for it contained the word "penis." The printers balked again. They were not covered for obscenity, so either they took a risk against possible prosecution, or else the word had to be removed, but that required an agreement from the group and they were all lost somewhere in the wilds of Canada. By a stroke of luck, Cleese returned to London and Geoffrey Strachan (the Methuen employee responsible for dealing with Python Productions) begged him to give consent to a change. Technically Idle was the editor, but Cleese took one look at the offending page and with a stroke of his pen substituted the words "brewer's droop" and that was the end of that.

The Python stage tours have always been a great release for the group; a celebration of idiocy. Free from the bonds of corporate censorship, surrounded by like-minded audience members, the group has always come alive on stage. There they would milk every bit of nuance from a gag, stretch a laugh until you thought you'd die of suspense waiting for the 16-ton weight to fall, the Colonel to interrupt, or for Cleese to proclaim "And now for something completely different!" Their stage tours were like a pop music concert, and the team was offering up "Monty Python's Greatest Skits" to a hungry crowd more than willing and able to finish a sketch for them should a member suddenly be struck down with amnesia. The Canadian / U.K. tour was especially liberating for Cleese who rediscovered the joys of performing live, but, high above the Atlantic, 31,000 feet above Canada, he announced a bombshell to the rest of the group: no more television. Period. On the surface the group seemed to accept his decision and his explanation: they had already done all there was to do on TV. What was the point, he wondered, in continuing? Deep down though, he says that some of the others felt less than diplomatic about his move. In fact they were downright nasty about it. Cleese felt that these unnamed people (Terry Jones) objected to his move out of an insecurity on their part in accomplishing things outside the group. Jones admits that he wasn't too thrilled at the prospect, but says that he was hardly as angry as Cleese believes.

For the moment though, everything was fine, and after a hard tour of Canada (playing dingy club halls one night and vast sports arenas the next) they returned to England to prepare for a season's fun at the Theatre Royal, Drury Lane. (This eventually became an LP, *Monty Python Live At Drury Lane* Charisma Class 4.) As the year wound down to a close, the BBC offered the group a fourth series. This was the cause of much trepidation, for without Cleese the team secretly wondered if the series would be as well received. Palin: "John brought to the series a certain middle-class indignation." Obviously the BBC was a little worried as well, for they suggested that only six episodes be commissioned (versus the normal 13) and they demanded that the words "Flying Circus" be dropped from the title. But uppermost in the minds of the executives at the BBC were the results of a BBC Audience Research Report which showed that a sizeable minority of Python fans agreed with John Cleese. They felt that the group was thrashing around, exploring the weird and strange rather than the funny.

So while the rest of the group made plans for the fourth series, Cleese busied himself with his newest venture, a film company he'd created with (Yes Minister co-author) Anthony Jay called Video Arts ("Business Movies That Make Business Better" reads their slogan), perhaps inspired by the industrials the group had made earlier in 1971. Gilliam also found time in 1972 to pan for the commercial dollar when he made a long animated film called *The Great Gas Gala* for the British Gas Board. Chapman, meanwhile, embarked on a project that would indirectly come back to haunt him and the rest of the group when, in 1972, he became co-founder of a homosexual newspaper called *Gay News*. (In 1976 the paper would print a poem by James Kirkup entitled "The Love That Dares To Speak Its Name" which was a fanciful description of a homosexual affair between a Roman Centurion and the crucified Jesus Christ. The publication of this poem led to a legal battle between the paper and the always indignant Mary Whitehouse on the grounds of blasphemy, and would later lead to many a legal and moral headache between Whitehouse and the Pythons when Monty Python's *Life of Brian* was released.)

The subject of homosexuality was always a subtopic in Python sketches; a submerged through-line in the narrative. Characters were either "pooves", or highly suspected of being them. And while they were nearly always portrayed as slightly mincing individuals, they were hardly ever the broad stereotypes drawn by rival comics of their time (Benny Hill comes to mind). This was mainly due to the group's respect for Chapman, and their strong belief that homosexuality was just another aspect of human society being kept under the thumb of those Whitehousian-type authorities, and one in need of liberation.

Chapman's homosexuality often left him as the "odd man out" within the group and, according to Graham, in one particularly sweet and funny instance, it made him the protagonist in a scenario that could have come directly out of a sketch. Often when filming on location the team would close out the day's activities by going out *en masse* to dinner, or to a night club, or to some other venue in order to unwind and have a laugh. On this particular occasion they had received news that there was a group of lovely young girls in a nearby village and, being the inquisitive types that they are, preparations were soon made to travel into town and see if these girls like the "English-type comedian." As they were getting ready to go, Chapman jokingly complained that "That might be alright for you lot, but what am I going to do?" That's when Terry Jones, a very sensitive, caring, and *decidedly heterosexual* man, walked up to Graham and, perhaps jokingly, offered to go to bed with him if it would make him feel better. According to Graham, he was at first astonished (*was* this a joke?), but then he became amused. Cautiously he told Terry that, while he appreciated the gesture, the simple truth of the matter was, well, he just didn't find Terry all that attractive. Graham said that Terry seemed to take this in stride, but, after a moment he stopped and in a hurt tone demanded to know "Why not?" Unable to elaborate on the point, or perhaps unwilling to, Graham said nothing. It is said that Terry Jones was no good to anyone the rest of that evening.

Monty Python's Fliegende Zircus

The Pythons produced two specials for Bavarian Television, one completely in German and the other in English. Below is a list of the sketches that appeared in the English-language version, subtitled "Schnapps With Everything." It was recorded entirely on film with no studio audience and was broadcast by the BBC on October 6th, 1973. Sections of this special were aired on Showtime in March 1990 as part of *20 Odd Years of Python*, a 20th anniversary salute to the team. Both specials were shown in their entirety by the Comedy Central comedy channel in January 1995. They were released on home video in 1998 by Guerilla Films.

"William Tell Quickie" / "Randy Financiers" / Opening titles / "Schliemer" / "Syncophancy" / "Mouse Ranch" / " Fish Reserve" / "Chicken Prospector" / "Huhnerminen von Nord-Dakota" / "Forged Chickens" / "Internationale Philosophis (a football match between Greek and German philosophers)" / "Self-wrestling" / "Philosophy Finale" / * "Traffic Noise" / "Ten Seconds of Sex" / "Hearing Aid and Contact Lens Shop" / "Happy Valley, or, The Princess with Wooden Teeth."

THE EPISODES

The episodes are listed in chronological order of original transmissions, with original transmission date, number in order of recording (in brackets) and date of recording (also in brackets). The transmission order of the first three series was different from the order in which they were recorded so that the best shows could be placed first and last in the series.

A few sketches were transferred to a different show after they were edited, and some shows have a subtitle. In most cases these subtitles were rejected names for the series, but not always. The series were recorded in two marathon sessions, which accounts for the dual dates under series headings. Compiling a running order for Monty Python's Flying Circus has been compared to trying to make a set of blueprints for a surrealist painting; the shows hardly ever have sketches that begin and end in the traditional sense. Consequently the details below are merely indications as to the content of a sketch.

Principal animation links are indicated by an asterisk (*), and are occasionally given titles, but, as they are usually more surreal than the sketches, even the team themselves soon gave up any hope of describing them in their scripts and just indicated where they should go.

The shows were written and performed entirely by Graham Chapman, John Cleese (except most of the fourth series), Eric Idle, Terry Jones, and Michael Palin. Special appearances are made by Carol Cleveland, Connie Booth, and Mrs. Idle (Eric's first wife). Animations and occasional appearances are by Terry Gilliam.

Interesting trivia surrounding the writing, performing or reception of a sketch is detailed in brackets {} at the end of each episode.

The group arrives in
America for a P.R.
tour, 1974. From
left: Terry Giliam,
Terry Jones, Graham
Chapman and Michael
Palin

THIRD SERIES

October 19, 1972-December 21, 1972
January 4, 1973-January 18, 1973

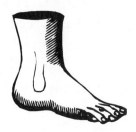

1: October 19, 1972 (5) (January 14, 1972):
"Multiple Murderer's Trial" / * "Man-hunt Inside a Man" / "Icelandic Saga" / Courtroom / * / "Stock Exchange Report" / * / "Mrs. Premise and Mrs. Conclusion visit Jean-Paul Sarte Alan Whicker Island".

{Malden, in "North Icelandic Saga", is referred to because it is a particularly uninteresting borough of London. There is something totally unscripted that happens off-camera during the "Courtroom Sketch" that cracks the team up – unfortunately no one remembers what it was. Idle's "Stock Exchange Report" was revamped years later on Saturday Night Live in a skit where Bill Murray describes the goings-on at a Clean Up New York's Porn Areas rally in erotic language. "Whicker's World" was first presented as an industrial film for Bird's Eye Frozen Foods. The idea of going to extreme lengths to prove a point, as Cleese and Chapman's characters did in "Mrs. Premise and Mrs. Conclusion", was revamped later by Woody Allen in his film *Annie Hall* where he settles a dispute between a couple in a movie line about Marshall McLuhan by actually going and dragging McLuhan from out of the queue.

2: October 26, 1972 (7) (January 28, 1972):

"Historic Emigration from Surbiton to Hounslow" / Opening titles / "Schoolboys Running Life Insurance Scams" / "How To Rid The World Of All Known Diseases" / "Mrs. Niggerbaiter Explodes" / "Vicar-Salesman" / "Farming Club" / "The Life of Tchaikovsky" / "Trim-Jeans Theatre" / "World War I" / "The BBC is Short of Money" / "Puss in Boots" / "It's".

Sharp eyes will notice a continuity error on Mr. Norris' historic journey to Hounslow, the diary pictured is indeed dated the 23rd-but of October, not April. There is a very obvious jab at the BBC's Paul Fox during ""The BBC is Short of Money" where *The Horse of the Year* show is mentioned as being one of the BBC's most popular programs. That show was often inserted in place of Python by the BBC. "It's" was the only time real guest stars appeared on the program. Ringo appeared as favor to Cleese and Chapman (they knew each other from *The Magic Christian*) and Lulu appeared because no one else was available. (Actually she was a big fan.) Chapman said that the idea behind this sketch was to finally give the Hermit an opportunity to finish the sentence that he'd been trying to say for years ("It's…"), of course, it didn't work out.

3: November 2, 1972 (1) (December 4, 1971):

"The Money Program" (including the song "There is nothing quite so wonderful as money") / Opening titles / "Erizabeth L" / "Fraud Film Squad" / * / "Salvation Fuzz" / * / "Jungle Restaurant" / "Apology for Violence" / "Nudity" / "Replacement with Gardening Club" / "Explorer's Club" / "The Lost World of Rolurama" / "Fraud Film Squad" / Closing titles / "Continuity trailer for six more minutes" / "Argument Clinic" / "Inspector Flying Fox of the Yard" / Continuity trailor for one more minute…

Notice that Chapman enters "Inspector's Sketch" as Inspector Fox of the Light Entertainment Police, Comedy Division, Special Flying (Circus) Squad. A dig at Paul Fox.

4: November 9, 1972 (2) (December 11, 1971):

"Blood, Devastation, Death, War and Horror" / "The Man who Speaks in Anagrams" / Opening titles (Tony M. Nyphot's Flying Riscu) / "Anagram Quiz" / "Merchant banker" / "Charity Appeal" / "Pantomime Horses" / "Life and Death Struggles" / * "The House Hunters" / "Mary Recruitment Office" / "Bus Conductor Sketch" / "City Gent who Makes People Laugh" / "Gestures to Indicate When a Televised Talk is Finished" / "Neurotic announcers" / TV news with Richard Baker (vision only, soundtrack continues with neurotic announcers) / "The Pantomime Horse Is A Secret Agent Film."

5: November 16, 1972 (9) (April 24, 1972):

"All-England Summarize Proust Competition" / Closing titles / "Everest Climbed by Hairdressers" / * "Romantic Film" / "Fire Brigade" / "Party Hints by Veronica" / * "Twelve Communist Revolutions" / "Language Laboratory" / "Travel Agent" / "Spanish Holiday Monologue" / "Theory on Brontosauruses".

The "Summarize Proust" sketch features an appearance by Roger McGough, ex-Scaffold member, as Superintendent McGough. (Scaffold was a "Pythonic" musical group, not unlike the Bonzo's, which also featured Paul McCartney's brother Michael) McGough is also the author of *Sporting Relations*, which was illustrated by Terry Gilliam. Notice that Idle hadn't quite worked out the punchline to his "Spanish Holiday" sketch here ("What a silly bunt"). The sketch appears later on their *Previous Record* LP intact. The character of Anne Elk is based on David Sherlock, who speaks in a roundabout manner. He didn't know this for many years until Chapman let it slip one day. He was a little upset about it.

6: November 23, 1972 (6) (January 21, 1972):

"Newsreel" / "Tory Housewives' Clean Up Campaign" / Opening titles / "Gumby Brain Specialist" / * / "'Live' documentary on mollusks" / * "Baby" / "News" / "The Minister For Not Listening To People" / "Tuesday

Documentary" / Children's story-Party political broadcast / "Politicians: an Apology" / "Naval Expedition to Lake Pahoe" / "The Silliest Interview we've Ever Had".

"Tory Housewives" was their non-too-subtle poke at the conservative faction that didn't like the show; as well as a dig at Mary Whitehouse and Margaret Thatcher. "Lake Pahoe" constitutes Chapman's other worst memory of doing the series. He was very drunk by the time they finally got around to filming this bit; it was cold and rainy and he had a very long monologue to remember and at one point he forgot entirely what he was to do next, but he eventually muddled through. It was during the filming of this sketch that he began to suspect that alcohol was starting to affect his work.

7: November 30, 1972 (4) (January 7, 1972):

"Biggles Dictates a Letter" / * / "Climbing the North Face of the Uxbridge Road" / "Lifeboat-Kitchen" / Old ladies with Electronic Snooping Equipment" / "Lifeboat" / "Storage Jars" / * "TV is Bad for Your Eyes" / "The Show so Far" / "Cheese Shop" / "'Philip Jenkinson' on Cheese Westerns" / Sam Peckinpah's "Salad Days" / Credit titles / "Apology" / "News Item with Richard Baker" / "Seashore Interlude" (2 minutes).

{Watch closely during "Biggles" as Chapman goofs at one point and begins to dictate without wearing the antlers. Gilliam's cartoon, "TV is bad for Your Eyes" is the one that supposedly offended Paul Fox. "Cheese Shop" was written out of desperation by Cleese and Chapman one day, a victim of their practice of staring at words in Roget's Thesaurus.}

8: December 7, 1972 (10) (May 4, 1972):

"The Cycling Tour" This is a continuous story where Mr. Pither (Palin) gets involved in road accidents / "The Russian Communist Party in Smolensk" / "The British Embassy run by Bingo-crazed Chinese" / and "A firing squad".

This show began life as a Palin / Jones script written for, and rejected by the BBC, and only became a Python script after Cleese, Idle and Chapman took it over and rewrote the last third. It was filmed entirely in Jersey, which also served to give the team a sort of vacation at the same time. It was the only episode to have a complete narrative–although several episodes in the fourth series, "Mr. Neutron" and "the Golden Age of Ballooning" –came very close.

9: December 14, 1972 (11) (May 11, 1972):

"Bomb on Plane" / "A Naked Man" / Opening titles / "Ten Seconds of Sex" / "Housing Project Built by Characters from 19th Century Literature" / "M1 Highway Built by Characters from Paradise Lost" / "Mystico and Janet" / "Flats Built Through Hypnosis" / "Mortuary Hour" / * / "Olympic Hide-and-Seek Finale" / "The Cheap-Laughs" / "Bull Fighting" / "The British Well-basically Club" / * / "Planet Algon" / Credits read out loud.

One of the people carrying the donkey at the end of "Olympic Hide and Seek" is Graham Chapman's adopted son John Tomiczek. "The Cheap-Laughs" goes nowhere fast and is really an odd combination of sketches: "Arthur Belling the Silly Vicar" and "Unwelcome Guests." It was just this sort of script derivation that was driving Cleese to distraction. "I could look at a sketch in the third series and see where it was a combination of other sketches," says Cleese. "A sketch from the first combined with one from the second but with a twist."

10: December 21, 1972 (13) (May 25, 1972):

"Tudor Jobs Agency" / "Dirty Books" / "Police Raid" / "Elizabethan Pornography Smugglers" / * / "Arthur Belling the Silly Vicar" / Opening titles / * / "The Free Repetition of Doubtful Words Skit" / "Is There?" / "The Man who has Problems with the Wrong Word Order" / "Thripshaw's Disease" / Silly noises / "Vicar-Sherry-Dirty Books" / Closing titles / Advert for Dr. E. Henry Thripshaw T-shirts.
The theme of sex and the church in this episode was later carried over into

print in *The Brand New Monty Python Bok* and the feature *Tits and Bums: A Weekly Look At Church Architecture*. Notice that in the "Is There?" sketch that Cleese is named Roger Last, after Python production designer Roger Last.

11: January 4, 1973 (8) (April 17, 1972):
"Boxing Tonight" / "Jack Bodell versus Sir Kenneth Clark" / Titles / "Dennis Moore" / "What the stars Foretel" / "Doctor" / * / "TV4 Or Not TV4?" / * "Victoria Regina" / "Dennis Moore" / "Lupins" / "Ideal Loon Exhibition" / "Off-License" / "Dennis Moore" / "Prejudice" / "Dennis Moore".

One of the patients in "Doctor" is Python film editor Ray Millichope. Jack Bodell is played by the same man who played Thom Jack, in the "Wrestling Epilog."

12: January 11, 1973 (3) (December 18, 1971):
"Party Political Broadcast" / "A Book at Bedtime" / "Red Gauntlet" read by dyslexic readers / "McKamikaze Scotsmen" / "No Time to Lose" / * "No-time Tolouse" / * "2001" / "The Intelligence of Penguins When Compared with BBC Program Planners" / "Unexploded Scotsman" / "Spot The Loony" Rival documentaries / Credits / trailer for "Dad's Doctors", "Dad's Pooves"

"Party Political Broadcast" was removed for repeats, which explains why the episode starts with captions. They also manage to get some extra mileage out of the 66-foot electric penguin from "Scott of the Antarctic" here.

13: January 18, 1973 (12) (May 18, 1972):
Thames TV intro / "Light Entertainment Awards" / "The Oscar Wilde Sketch" / * "Powder my Nose" / * "Charwoman" / "David Niven's Fridge" / Pasolini's film "Cricket Match" / "A New Brain From Curry's" / "Blood

Donors" / "International Wife Swapping" / Credits of the Year / "The Dirty Vicar Sketch".

Idle is amazing in this episode with his Richard Attenborough impersonation which, like most of this episode, was written by Cleese and Chapman. This episode reflected their then-current attitude towards the film business. "The Oscar Wilde Sketch" was written mainly by Chapman because he and Sherlock were writing a film on Wilde at the time (it was never completed). Notice that "International Wife Swapping" features, at one point, everyone dancing to the song "Brazil"–later an important tune for Terry Gilliam. The "New Brain from Curry's" sketch features the scene of Cleese holding what the BBC thought was a giant penis. In fact it's a severed arm.

At the author's urgings,
the above photo has been
omitted. It was originally
a photo of him, but vanity
won out and we cut it.

THE BEST LINES FROM THE THIRD SERIES

IDLE has been accused of murdering over 20 people, and JONES, the judge, asks if he has anything to say:

IDLE: Yes, sir. I'm very sorry.

JONES: (disbelievingly) You're very sorry.

IDLE: Yes sir. It was a very bad thing to have done and I'm really very ashamed of myself. I can only say it won't happen again.

IDLE is giving us a stock exchange report:

IDLE: Trading was crisp at the start of the day with some brisk business on the floor. Rubber hardened and string remained confident. Little bits of tin consolidated although biscuits sank after an early gain and stools remained anonymous… After lunch naughty things dipped sharply, forcing giblets upwards with the knicky knacky knoo….

CLEESE and CHAPMAN are two PEPPERPOTS:

CHAPMAN: Busy day?

CLEESE: Busy? I just spent four hours burying the cat.

CHAPMAN: Four hours to bury a cat?

CLEESE: Yes… it wouldn't keep still… wiggling about…

CHAPMAN: Oh, it wasn't dead, then?

CLEESE: No no, but it's not an at all well cat. So, as we are going away for a fortnight I thought I'd better bury it. Just to be on the safe side.

CHAPMAN: Quite right. You don't want to come back from Sorento to a dead cat. It'd be so anti-climatic. Yes, kill it now I say.

JONES, in drag, asks her husband IDLE what he wants with his jugged fish:

IDLE: Halibut.

JONES: The jugged fish is halibut.

IDLE: Well what fish have you got that isn't jugged, then?

JONES: Rabbit.

IDLE: What, rabbit fish?

JONES: Yes… it's got fins.

IDLE: Is it dead?

JONES: Well it was coughing-up blood last night!

CHAPMAN, their son, enters and says that "there's a dead Bishop on the landing":

JONES: Where did that come from?

CHAPMAN: What do you mean?

JONES: What's its diocese?

CHAPMAN: Well it looked a bit Bath and Wellsish to me.

IDLE goes out to have a look, and re-enters:

IDLE: Leicester.

JONES: How'd you know?

IDLE: Tattooed on the back of the neck.

CLEESE is having a paid argument with PALIN, yet he refuses to continue unless PALIN pays some more. PALIN insists that he's already paid:

PALIN: Aha! Well, if I didn't pay you then why
           are arguing? Got you!

CLEESE: Not necessarily. I could be arguing in
           my spare time.

IDLE speaks in anagrams:

PALIN: I believe you're working on an anagram
           version of Shakespeare?

IDLE: that si crreoct. Ta the mnemot I'm
           working on The Mating of the Wersh.

PALIN: The Mating of the Wersh? By William
           Shakespeare?

IDLE: Nay, by Malliwi Rapesheake.

PALIN: And what is your next project?

IDLE: Ring Kichard the Thrid.

PALIN: Ah, Ring Kichard… But surely that's not
           an anagram, that's a Spoonerism.

IDLE: (upset) If you're going to split hairs
           I'm going to piss off.

CHAPMAN is a contestant trying to summarize
Proust's masterwork, A la Rechereche du Temps Perdu
in 15 seconds:

JONES: What are your hobbies, outside summa-
           rizing?

CHAPMAN: Well, strangling animals… golf, and
           masturbating.

CLEESE is trying to buy some cheese from cheese shop owner PALIN. Unfortunately he's out of every cheese imaginable—yet he insists to CLEESE that his shop is the finest in the district:

CLEESE: And what leads you to that conclusion?

PALIN: Well, it's so clean.

CLEESE: It's certainly uncontaminated by cheese.

PALIN is Mr. Pither, who's on a cycling tour of North Cornwall. He's at a hospital, giving his name to CHAPMAN, a nurse:

PALIN: Ah, My name is Pither. P-i-t-h-e-r. As in brotherhood except for the p-i instead of the b-r-o and no hood.

PALIN is a man who speaks in the wrong word order:

CLEESE: Tell me more about your problem.

PALIN: Well, as I say, you'll just be talking and out will pudential the wrong word, and ashtray's you uncle. I'm awfully strawberry about it.

CLEESE: Upset.

PALIN: It's so embarrassing when my wife and I go to an orgy.

CLEESE: A party?

PALIN: No, an orgy. We live in Esher.

CLEESE is Dennis Moore, trying to convince passengers on the Lupin Express that he's a good shot:

CLEESE: I practice every day. Well not absolutely every day, I mean most days in the week. I expect I must practice four… or five times a week. At least. At least four or five. Only some weekends, like last weekend, there really wasn't much time so that moves the average down a bit. But I should say it's definitely a solid four days practice every week. At least. I mean, I reckon I could hit that tree over there, the one behind the hillet. Not the big hillet, the little one on the left. You see the three trees? The third tree from the left in back of it. That one. I reckon I could hit that… four times out of five. On a good day. With this wind, seven times out of ten.

THE FOURTH SERIES

"MORE BEANS!!"

From the 4th series.
John had already
left. From left:
Terry Jones, Michael
Palin, Terry Giliam,
Eric Idle and
Graham Chapman.

THE FOURTH SERIES

Oct. 31, 1974-Dec. 5, 1974

The Pythons spent the majority of 1973 thinking about film. Their successful stage tour completed, they returned to England with a vague notion of doing another movie and immediately began writing. Rather, they immediately began typing–for without a solid plot to hang their dialog on, the first draft of their film (tentatively called *Monty Python's Second Film*) was merely a collection of vaguely related sketches. Frustrated, they abandoned the project to concentrate instead on what was turning out to be a popular (and profitable) venue for them: comedy LPs.

The comedy record experienced something of a resurgence of popularity in the early '70s. Although comics had been making them ever since the invention of the special Rubber Chicken Latex needed to press them on, the popularity of the medium soared to unprecedented heights in the early part of the decade. Every comic worth his seltzer made one: Cheech and Chong, George Carlin, The Firesign Theatre, Freddie Prinze and, of course, Python. Perhaps this popularity is traceable to the audience's desire to own a part of their favorite TV show or group; it was certainly one of the only ways to replay your favorite jokes or sketches over and over as the use of VCRs was still some 10 years off. Regardless, the medium flourished and Python was a consumer favorite.

Their approach to the comedy LP was similar to The Firesign Theatre's in that it was usually a multi-track recording with layers upon layers of ideas, sound effects, and dialog piled high on top of each other. It was the aural equivalent to their television program; a very visual approach, almost "theatre of the mind." Consequently their LPs bear up to repeated listenings as you always hear something you missed the first time around.

In late September 1973, the group recorded *Matching Tie and Handkerchief*, their *Sgt. Pepper's*. Aside from being, perhaps, the funniest of their LPs, *Matching Tie and Handkerchief* (Charisma CAS 1080) featured the novel idea of interlaced grooves. This meant that there were two sets of grooves on side 2 (there were also two side twos) and it was merely a matter of luck which side played when you set the needle down. Although the idea had been done on 78s as early as 1911, the Pythons were the first to employee it on long playing records. (The idea had been Terry Jones'.) The album's producer, Andrew Jacquemin, has later claimed that the idea had been proposed for *Monty Python's Previous Record*, but technical difficulties prevented it. *Matching Tie and Handkerchief* also proved to be the catalyst that introduced Monty Python to the lucrative U.S. college market, accomplishing the job that *And Now For Something Completely Different* failed to do. The LP became an immediate success on college radio, the medium through which most "underground" groups (musical and otherwise) gain national exposure.

The success of the LP (it reached #49 on the U.K. charts) prompted the group to visit America where they appeared (sans Cleese) on *The Tonight Show*, with guest host Joey Bishop. The three-martini-and-golf set of *The Tonight Show* was perhaps the last place the Pythons needed to appear. They came on and did a lot of Pepperpot routines, much to the bafflement of the studio audience who seemed ill at ease with these men in drag with their screeching English accents. Needless to say, the group was not asked to sit and chat with Joey. Later they appeared on *The Midnight Special*, a limp, youth-oriented rock music show that featured the disc jockey Wolfman Jack as its host. They fared a little better. Success in America was building. Slowly. The team returned to England to resume work on their film script, now being called *Monty Python and the Holy Grail*, as they latched onto an idea of Michael Palin's about King

Arthur. Their abandoned first draft would not go unused though as many of its best ideas were later to appear in the fourth series as sketches. (The film script for both the abandoned first draft and the shooting script for *Holy Grail* were later turned into *Monty Python and the Holy Grail* (Book) Methuen 1977. It was edited by Terry Jones.)

By now Monty Python, (both the troupe and the series) was an extremely popular entity in the United Kingdom and, cautiously, the BBC offered them a fourth series. The team (sans Cleese) agreed to do it, but first they had other projects to complete. They appeared for a season's run at the Drury Lane Theatre in March of 1974 (with Cleese), then immediately began filming of *Holy Grail* in Scotland (also with Cleese. He was happy to appear on stage or on film with them, just not on television.)

Their past experience in film prompted them to find a producer a little more simpatico to work with this time around, so they tapped Mark Forstater for the job. Theatrical impresario Michael White, who had been responsible for bringing *Cleese and Chapman's Cambridge Circus* revue to London's West End in 1963 was responsible for finding backing for the project.

He tapped what was, at that time, an odd source: rock groups. Bands like Pink Floyd, Jethro Tull, and Led Zeppelin were more than willing to help put up the modest $500,000 needed to put the story on the screen. A similar scenario transpired when the group needed funding for their next film, *Monty Python's Life of Brian*, when their original backer, Lord Delfont, backed all the way out of the project and ex-Beatle George Harrison stepped in. (Brian became the first film for the newly-formed Handmade Films company.) There has always been an affinity between rock musicians and comics. The going theory is that rockers want to be funny and that comics want to be able to attract the same sort of girls that the rockers attract.

So with the formation of their own film company, Python (Monty) Pictures, filming for *Holy Grail* began in mid-1974 in the remote Scottish highlands and was almost immediately plagued with problems. Graham Chapman, who was by this time a full-fledged alcoholic, began to suffer the horrors of the D.T.s on the very first day of shooting. Chapman said, "I actually began to go through the D.T.s at the start of *Holy Grail*, actually before the first shot, the one where King Arthur has to cross over the Bridge of Death and Eternal Peril. The irony was not lost on me." He kept himself "topped-up" with huge quantities of alcohol throughout the rest of filming and he made a vow then and there to give up drinking forever. (He made good on his promise some two years later and remained dry until his death in 1989.) Problems also arose because "Democracy gone mad" dictated that the film have not one, but two directors, Terry Jones and Terry Gilliam. Jones (who had taken a BBC director's course years earlier and had, in fact, co-direct several Python episodes with MacNaughton) remembers the film fondly, although he says it had "a loopy schedule" where things that should have taken a minute took all day, and bits that should have taken a week (The Knights Who Say "Ni!") were done in a single day. Terry Gilliam (who directed his own film inserts for Python episodes) was less than happy with the dual directors arrangement. But the end result is a film that quite remarkably captures the look and feel of medieval Britain considering the film's budget restraints. The budget was so tight that, even though the group deferred their fees until such a time as the film went into profits (which it did a year later), most of the original sound-track (specially composed by Neil Innes) had to be scrapped and stock music from DeWolfe had to be used.

By this time Neil Innes had unofficially joined the team as the "seventh mad musical Python," even accompanying them as a warm-up act on their stage tours. Preparations were soon made to begin recordings for the fourth series, but things were still changing at the BBC. New and harsher restraints were being placed on their programs, and they were more willing to admit to the existence of censorship within the Corporation. But, they pleaded, if we don't do it, "outside sources" will demand it. These "outside sources" were never named, but I imagine that if you were to shout out the name Mary Whitehouse you'd get a good old Shropshire-accented "You-hoo!" in response. The BBC was becoming top-heavy with conservative-minded executives, all being placed under long contract, while the creative types were being given short term leases, all heavily peppered with restrictions. New budget restraints were also in effect at the Beeb, forcing the group to record only the amount of film needed to do an episode and no more. (In the past they had always recorded some five to ten minutes over time so that they could control the pacing better in the editing process.) The BBC also demanded that the shows start as soon as possible, thus negating the Pythons practice of reshuffling the episodes so that the best appeared first and last in the series. They went out as they were filmed. The BBC also demanded that the show be renamed simply "Monty Python".

Over the years there has been much heated debate in Python circles over the fourth series. Some say that the quality of material is weak and strained, while others claim that it is brilliant. The team itself received quite a critical drubbing at the time and, as a whole, the series is not as well liked by the fans. However, on a personal note I'd like to say that I find the fourth series fascinating and as good in many ways as the best of what preceded it. The writing (while not always successful) is at a razor's sharpness and the infamous "stream-of-consciousness" effect is at its most heightened. According to Graham Chapman, a conscious effort was made at the time to give each episode a single narrative line (although it may be a far-fetched one), so that the end result is like the "tumbling bad dream" effect they are so noted for. This was due to two factors: 1) The left-over sketch ideas from the abandoned first draft of *Holy Grail*, which already had something of a narrative, and 2) The fact that the group was getting increasingly fed up with television and were already thinking in the longer narrative, with an eye toward movies.

The fourth series had its problems though. Terry Gilliam had less time to work on animations, what with the stepped-up timetable of transmissions, and Eric Idle wrote very little. Eric Idle. Although Eric is a consummate performer, talented musician, and an excellent impressionist, his overall script output in Monty Python does seem hardly equal in volume to the Cleese / Chapman and the Palin / Jones contributions. Why is this? Being the lone writer in the group, it's quite possible that Eric lost a good many "battles of inclusion" during writing-meetings as he had no allies to help him fight for his material. Or perhaps it's because Eric preferred to spread his considerable talents more across the board, into song writing and acting. Or, perhaps it's because (as Graham once remarked) "Eric likes his holidays." (We may never know. When recently questioned as to why his script contributions for the fourth series were so slim, Eric's reply was: "Who knows, who cares, who gives a shit?") Regardless, Idle's output was slim during the fourth series which contributed to the overall feeling that the team was breaking up. Indeed, they soon realized what Cleese had said a series earlier: They had already done all there was to do on TV. Eric was especially having second-thoughts about continuing. Idle: "We did six episodes, and then the BBC wanted another seven and at that point I said 'no!' Michael tried to talk me into it, but I said 'It's just not working.' There was this lovely tension between John and Terry (Jones)—I mean, there was a series of balances and tensions-that allowed the show to work. Without the full group it never worked quite as well."

In October, the same month that the first episode of the fourth series aired, Cleese and Connie Booth made a film, based on a Chekov story, entitled *Romance With A Double Bass*. It is mainly notable for the fact that they both spent the majority of the picture in the nude. Cleese admits that he didn't see all of the fourth series episodes of Python at the time, but says that his general impression was that "they weren't all that good." Without Cleese and Jones locking horns in the writing-meetings the scripts were said to be too one-dimensional; that Jones appeared to be bulldozing his ideas through as there was no one there willing to put up too much of a fight against him. Cleese did contribute, although indirectly, to a couple of the fourth series episodes when some material about ants that he'd written with Chapman (mainly *Holy Grail* out takes) were used.

During Cleese's absence, Chapman wrote a bit with Palin and Neil Innes, and he even wrote one sketch with Douglas (*A Hitchhiker's Guide To The Galaxy*) Adams. John Tomiczek recalls that Adams (who was fresh from Cambridge Footlights) had suddenly appeared on the scene around the close of the third series, usually parking his caravan (trailer) outside the BBC, and followed the team whenever they went on location, volunteering to do any odd bit parts that came up. Tomiczek also recalled that Douglas was not at all shy about proposing sketch ideas of his own and that he was also a bit of a magpie; assimilating any stray ideas that the Pythons had rejected. He particularly recalls Adams using an idea that they had tossed about a haddock enrolling in Eton College, and says that a lot of his second Hitchhiker book, *The Restaurant At The End Of The Universe*, came from an abandoned television script Adams and Chapman had worked on called *The Ringo Starr Show*.

On December 12th, 1974, the very last episode on Monty Python was transmitted by the BBC. Tired of the constant battles with the Beeb over censorship, and seemingly unable to breakout in America, the team went their own separate ways. That same December, Cleese recorded the pilot episode of another series called *Fawlty Towers* that would prove to become one of the most popular in British TV history (This was later to be adapted, adopted and yet not improved when it was transferred to America by ABC as a show called *Amanda's By The Sea*, starring Bea (*Maude, The Golden Girls*) Arthur. Also starring, as the Manuel clone named Aldo, was Tony Rosato who would later star on *SCTV* and *Saturday Night Live*). Meanwhile, Chapman fell back to scripting episodes of *Doctor In The House*, Idle wrote a novel (*Hello Sailor*, Futura 1976), a radio series (*Radio 5*) and a very funny (though rarely seen) TV series called *Rutland Weekend Television*, with Neil Innes. (It later spawned *The Rutles.*) Palin and Jones also wrote a book (*Bert Fegg's Nasty Book For Boys and Girls*. Later published as *Dr. Fegg's Nasty Book of Knowledge* and still later published as *Dr. Fegg's Encyclopedia of All World Knowledge*), as well as TV play entitled *Secrets*. The team began to settle down, little suspecting the uproar of delight that was waiting around the corner when in July, 1974, KERA-TV in Dallas began showing reruns of *Monty Python's Flying Circus*. It was about to start all over again.

On the set of
'Brian.' Graham and
longtime companion,
David Sherlock,
share a laugh.

THE EPISODES

The fourth series, the last series of half hour shows that the team did for the BBC, was substantially different from the preceding three in many ways. First and foremost, they were transmitted in the same order that they were recorded. This was due to many factors, the most significant being that the BBC's period of unbridled expansion was now over. The group was placed on a tight schedule that left little room for experimentation, or for many of those expensive Palin and Jones films. Much of the previous three series' manic energy was due to the fact that the shows were recorded some five minutes over time, thus allowing them a chance to play with the pacing in the editing room. No more. All fourth series shows were filmed to time.

Also, John Cleese was now gone. At least from the day to day grind of filming and writing (some of his material found its way into the fourth series). This worried the BBC, as they felt that he had become somewhat of a draw for viewers (in much the same way Chevy Chase's departure on *Saturday Night Live* bothered the executives at NBC). Consequently the BBC commissioned only six shows. As if to signal that the mix wasn't quite right, the name was also shortened to *Monty Python*. (The "Flying Circus" part remained a copyright of the BBC for many years. Today the words "Monty Python", "Python" and "Flying Circus" belong to Python (Monty) Pictures.)

We ran out of pic-
tures. Feel free to
paste one in of
yourself.

THE FOURTH SERIES

October 31, 1974-December 5, 1974

1: "The Golden Age of Ballooning" October 31, 1974 (1) (October 12, 1974):
This is a continuous story involving the Montgolfier Brothers and George III.

I can't help but notice how much Chapman, as George III, looks like Jeffrey Jones as the Emperor in Amadeus. Or rather, vice versa. This episode also features a song by Neil Innes called "George III".

2: "Michael Ellis" November 7, 1974 (2) (October 19, 1974):
Opening titles / Closing titles /" Department store" / "Buying an Ant" / "At Home With the Ant" / TV show on ants / "Department Store" / "Poetry reading" / "Toupee Hall" / different endings.

The majority of this episode was written by Cleese and Chapman, for *Holy Grail*, and the scripts can be found in their book *Monty Python and the Holy Grail* (Book). Chapman took their sketches, rewrote them, and presented them to the team. There are many references in the fourth series to Norway for some reason.

3. "Light Entertainment War" November 14, 1974 (3) (October 26, 1974):

"Up Your Pavement" / Biographical introductions / "RAF Station 1944" (banter) / "Trivialising the War" / "Court martial" / "Anything Goes In" (song) / Film trailer / Opening titles / "The Public Are Idiots" / "The Last Five Miles of the M1" / Program titles conference / * "What a Horrible Day" / "Woody and Tinny Words" / Program title show-jumping / Newsflash (Germans) / "When Does A Dream Begin" (song).

For many years this episode was tied-up in litigation (because of securing rights to the Innes song, "When Does A Dream Begin?") and was never re-broadcast. It was broadcast in January 1995 on the Comedy Central cable network, so perhaps everything's been worked out. Innes is singing the song here to Gilliam's wife, Maggie, who did make-up on the series.

4: "Hamlet" November 21, 1974 (4) (November 2, 1974):

"Bogus Psychiatrists" / "Nationwide" / "Police-Helmets" / "Father-in-Law" / Opening titles / "Hamlet" / * / "After Boxing Match" / "Shopping (Mrs. Gorilla)" / "A Room at Polonius's House" / (sports results) / "Dentists" / "Race from Epsom" / "European Cup".

Most of the sketches in this episode can be found in *Monty Python and the Holy Grail* (Book). Lots of references to Queen Victoria, referees, and Norway in the fourth series.

5: "Mr. Neutron" November 28, 1974 (5) (November 9, 1974):

More or less a continuous story about Mr. Neutron (Chapman), post office boxes, a CIA agent named Teddy Salad, and an agent disguised as a dog.

Watch for *Hitchhiker* author Douglas Adams at the beginning as one of the Pepperpots bringing Idle their old missiles. Sharp eyes will notice that the issue of *Radio Times* which Idle holds is the October 26th edition, featuring Python on its cover.

6: "Party Political Broadcast" December 12, 1974 (6) (November 16, 1974):
"The Most Awful Family In Britain" / "Icelandic Honey Week" / Opening titles / "A Doctor" / "Brigadier and the Bishop" / * / "Appeal on Behalf of Extremely Rich People" / "The Man who Finishes Other People's Sentences / "The Walking Tree of Dahomey" / "The Batsmen of the Kalahari" / Credits / BBC News.

"A Doctor" was written by Chapman and Douglas Adams. Notice that the portrait hanging in his office is of BBC Head of Light Entertainment, Bill Cotton. There's a rather in-joke made at one point during "The Walking Tree of Dahomey" where Palin refers to a tree as Bornous Bamber Gascoignous. Bamber Gascoigne was (is) a semi-legendary actor / comedian from the 1950s well-known to Cambridge students. He also wrote the introduction to Roger Wilmut's book *From Fringe To Flying Circus.*

Terry Gilliam artwork

THE BEST LINES FROM THE FOURTH SERIES

JONES and CHAPMAN are PEPPERPOTS:

JONES: Morning Mrs. Smoker.

CHAPMAN: Morning Mrs. Non-smoker.

JONES: What, have you been shopping?

CHAPMAN: No, I've been shopping.

JONES: What'd you buy?

CHAPMAN: A piston engine.

JONES: What'd you buy that for?

CHAPMAN: It was a bargain.

JONES: Well how much do you want for it?

CHAPMAN: Three quid.

JONES: (handing CHAPMAN imaginary bills)
            Done!...How do you cook it?

CHAPMAN: You don't cook it.

JONES: (pointing to piston engine) Well you can't eat that raw!

CHAPMAN is Mr. Neutron visiting PALIN (in drag) and JONES.

PALIN is telling him all about the family

PALIN: Then there's Stanley, our eldest. He's a bio-chemist in Sudbury. He's married to Shirley-

CHAPMAN: Shirley who used to be a hairdresser?

PALIN: That's right. She's a lovely person- mind, my husband thinks she's a bit...flash

JONES: (sullen) I hate her. I hate her guts.

PALIN: They come down most weekends so you'll get to meet them.

CHAPMAN: I'd love to. Hairdressing is very inter- esting.

PALIN: Ooh, it's very important too! If you don't care for your scalp you get rabies!

IDLE is a Brigadier dictating a letter to PALIN, a Bishop. He realizes that he feels strong emotions towards PALIN:

IDLE: Brian, let's stop all this pretending, shall we?

PALIN: Yes, as Dirk Bogarde said in his auto-biography—

IDLE: Brian... let's stop all this futile pretense. I've... I've always been moderately fond of you...

PALIN: Well, to be quite frank Brigadier...one can't walk so closely with a chap like you for... so long without... feeling something... deep down inside... even if isn't anything... anything very much.

IDLE: Well, splendid Brian!... I don't suppose there's much that we can do, really.

PALIN: Not on television, no.

JONES and IDLE are the Montgolfier brothers, about to ascend in the first hot-air balloon, 1783 in Annonay, France:

JONES: It is a great moment for France! The first ascent in a hot-air balloon by the Montgolfier brothers, 1783. I can see us now... just after Montague and just before Mozart!

IDLE: I think I'll go and wash.

JONES: Good luck!

IDLE: Oh it's quite easy really. I just slap a little water on my face.

IDLE has bought an ant from clerk PALIN:

IDLE: What do you feed them on?

PALIN: Blancmange.

IDLE: Blancmange?

PALIN: Sorry , don't know why I said that. No, you don't feed them at all.

IDLE: Well what do they live on?

PALIN: They don't, they die.

IDLE: They die?

PALIN: Of course they do if you don't feed them.

IDLE: I don't understand.

PALIN: Well you let them die. Then you buy another one. It's cheaper than feeding them and that way you have a constant variety of little companions. That's the advantage of owning an ant!

IT WAS 30-ODD YEARS AGO LAST WEEK: THE PYTHONS ON PYTHON

"Python was really writing and arguing for three hours. Typewriters were thrown, people would storm out of rooms, there'd be shrill voices—all of which was important for the writing process."
– MICHAEL PALIN

"I think I only threw a chair at John once." – TERRY JONES

"I used to have a lot of fights with Terry Jones, but they were basically artistic fights… the two of us used to lock antlers a great deal but it actually worked extremely well because we sort of neutralized each other."
– JOHN CLEESE

"There was this lovely tension between John and Terry… there were a series of tensions and balances that allowed Python to work, and without the full group it never worked as well."
– ERIC IDLE

"I think that all of us, fortunately, were able to subjugate to a large extent our personal feelings and personal hurts, as well, because the end result was created by Python, the group, rather than Python the individuals."
–GRAHAM CHAPMAN

"I think we all got on astonishingly well." –JOHN CLEESE

"John was the head and Terry (Jones) was the heart of Python."
–MICHAEL PALIN

"I think what Python introduced, or accentuated, in comedy, was aggression. I think that was very much John's input there."
–TERRY JONES

"John, luckily, is very visual – as a human being – it would be very difficult to draw something as funny as that."
–TERRY GILLIAM

"I wouldn't persay say there was any subject at all that I wouldn't immediately think of not making jokes about."
–JOHN CLEESE

"The thing that makes me squirm the most about that first series is some of the camp stereotypes…the sort of limp-wristed…camp stereotypes – which we wouldn't do now."
–TERRY JONES

"At times we were making the characters more and more cartoon-like. Things got stranger and stranger."
–TERRY GILLIAM

"There was a sort of competition within the group. A certain amount of angling, politicking for roles. I suppose in some respects that I felt, as co-author with John of many scenes, that when it came to casting that perhaps I should have had a role where Michael would get the role. Nobody would think of me as having written, say, The Dead Parrot because most people know it as John and Michael."
–GRAHAM CHAPMAN

"There's still a lot of competitiveness in the group. We all want the others to do well – but we don't want them to produce total masterpieces because that would be rather annoying."

–JOHN CLEESE

"We were actually very conscious of not trying to be satirical and topical. I think a silly election is always going to be a silly election."

–TERRY GILLIAM

"There was a corporate consciousness in the group."

–GRAHAM CHAPMAN

"There was only one thing that we all agreed on, and that was that the show would never work in America."   –ERIC IDLE

"We were treated like pop stars in America. It was quite incredible."

–CAROL CLEVELAND

"It would be very difficult to all get back together again. For a start we're all older and fatter, more lined … it would be a bit pathetic."

–TERRY JONES

"Python represents a period of my life which was great fun and rather painful at times. I think I would enjoy it more if I were to do it all again (now that I'm sober)."

–GRAHAM CHAPMAN

"I think people are happier now to just be friends without the pressure of felling that you have to get something done next. That we've got to reform. But really, we never sort of had greedy managers or people saying 'Come on lads, you've got to get out there and do another show. Money money money…' I mean the greed has come from within the group."

–MICHAEL PALIN

"I like what I'm doing now. I've done Python. It's past."
                                        –TERRY GILLIAM

"We just used to hoot in delight when we thought of some other silly thing we could do."
                                        –JOHN CLEESE

THE HITCHHIKER'S GUIDE TO MONTY PYTHON AND DOUGLAS ADAMS

Douglas Adams' involvement in Monty Python has been exaggerated to say the least. Not by Adams mind you, but by the American promotions group responsible for his first book, *A Hitchhiker's Guide to the Galaxy*. No, Adams would be one of the first to tell you that his association with the Pythons was hardly the break of a lifetime that one would imagine; in fact it was a failure that left the then 24-year old writer feeling like his career was over before it had even begun.

Douglas Adams' association with Python began during their controversial fourth series. John Cleese was now gone, leaving Graham Chapman without a permanent writing partner, and he was on the lookout for new talent. The Footlights revue that year was called *Chox*, and it was the first Cambridge revue to make it to London's West End in many a year. Chapman had heard great things about the show and went to check it out. He liked what he saw, especially the work of a 22-year-old Cambridge graduate named Douglas Adams. He invited him over to the bar for a drink. This eventually led to many drinks and the beginnings of a writing partnership that was to last the next eighteen months. One of the first projects that they wrote for was Monty Python. Since both of them had some background in medicine, they decided to write a doctor skit. The result was called "A Doctor" and was a vicious satire that involved Terry Jones as a man bleeding to death in the doctor's office, forced to fill out a sheaf of meaningless quizzes on history and auto racing, before the doctor, Chapman, would treat him. It was gory, mean-spirited and extremely funny. Adams then had a walk-on in the "Mr. Neutron" episode, as a Pepperpot off-loading a bunch of old missiles. His final contribution to the team was on their *Holy Grail* soundtrack. He co-wrote the heavily re-written sketch about a film director whose latest movie is said to star the long-dead Marilyn Monroe.

Separate from Python, he and Chapman wrote a number of one-off projects including "Out Of The Trees", a TV sketch show that starred Chapman and Simon Jones. ("My favorite bit from that show," Adams says, "is a sketch about Genghis Khan. He has become so powerful that he hardly has time for conquering anymore, and he spends all his time with financial planners. It's based somewhat loosely on strange mutterings Graham made at the time, complaints about how successful the Pythons had become.") "Out Of The Trees" had one, unannounced, airing then promptly disappeared from sight. (A second episode, never filmed, included the sketch about a haddock enrolling at Eton. This is the idea that John Tomiczek later claimed that Adams pilfered from rejected Python material.)

The Chapman / Adams pair also created a show called *The Ringo Starr Show*. It never even got past the scripting stage. This is unfortunate, as this show had perhaps the most interesting premise of all of them. It was a sci-fi comedy show that had Ringo playing a chauffeur who carried his boss around on his back. Then, one day a flying saucer lands and gives Ringo amazing super powers, such as the ability to travel through space, destroy the universe by waving his hand (much like Mr. Neutron), as well as the ability to do flower arranging. It was supposed to be a one hour American TV special, but this deal (like most Chapman / Adams projects) fell through. Adams did manage to save one idea from it, the Golafrincham B-Ark sequence, which he later used in his *Hitchhiker's book*. ("Without," stressed John Tomiczek, "co-crediting the idea to Graham.") The Chapman / Adams partnership finally dissolved during the writing of Chapman's autobiography, *A Liar's Autobiography*. Adams freely admits that the two had problems co-writing it ("nearly came to blows over it," says Adams), and Chapman said that his complaint was that Adams was "trying to take the book over, although it was probably done unconsciously."

While the pair decided against any future collaboration, they did remain friends, and talk of reviving *The Ringo Starr Show* continued to raise its head up until Chapman's death from cancer in 1989.

More Terry Gilliam
artwork

(HIGHLY EDITED, LESS ANAL)

THE
MONTY PYTHON
BIBLIOGRAPHY

By Hans Ten Cate
(c)1998-99 Hans Ten Cate
(See the totally anal, absolutely complete
Monty Python Bibliography at: www.dailyllama.com)
Used by permission

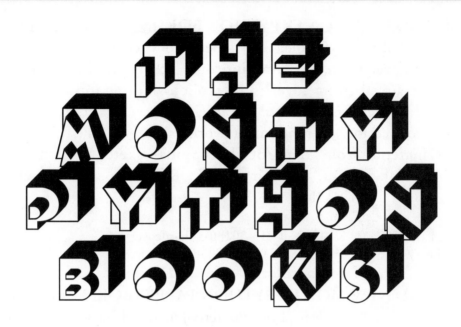

MONTY PYTHON'S BIG RED BOOK, by (in a rather silly order as in the book) Michael Palin, Eric Idle, Graham Chapman, Terry Jones, John Cleese, and the Illustrated Terry Gilliam

    (Monty Python's first book contains a random assortment of silly compositions, including Terry Gilliam's art work and references to many of the popular sketches such as the "Lumberjack Song", the "Whizzo Chocolate Assortment", "Silly Walks", the "Poems of Ewan McTeagle", and the "Piranha Brothers"; edited by Eric Idle; actually has a blue cover)

Methuen, 1971 (U.K.) SBN 416-66890-9 (hardcover)
Warner Books, 1975 (U.S.) ISBN 0-446-87077-3 (***)
Methuen, 1972, 1973, 1974, 1975, 1976, 1979, 1980, 1982, 1984, 1986 (U.K.) ISBN 0-413-29520-6 (paperback)
Mandarin Paperbacks, 1991, 1993 (U.K.) 0-7439-1173-8 (paperback)

THE BRAND NEW MONTY PYTHON BOK, by Graham Chapman, John Cleese, Terry Gilliam, Eric Idle, Terry Jones, and Michael Palin (the hardcover version has a plain white dust jacket with the correct title on it while the actual front cover is an explicit photograph of three nude women and is titled *Tits 'n' Bums: A Weekly Look at Church Architecture;* the book is a collection of random artwork, sketches, and photographs; includes material from some of the popular sketches such as "Sam Peckinpah's Salad Days, the Fairy Tale", 'Rat Recipes", "Travel Agent sketch"; edited by Eric Idle)

Methuen, 1973, 1974 (U.K.) ISBN 0-413-30130-3 (hardcover)
Henry Regnery Co., 1976 (U.S.) ISBN 0-8092-8046-9 (hardcover)

THE BRAND NEW MONTY PYTHON PAPPERBOK, by Michael Palin, Graham Chapman, John Cleese, Eric Idle, Terry Jones, and Terry Gilliam (contents are identical to the hardcover edition except there is no "Tits and Bums" cover)

Methuen, 1974, 1975, 1976, 1979, 1980, 1983, 1986 (U.K.) ISBN 0-413-31970-9 (paperback)
Warner Books, 1976 (U.S.) ISBN 0-446-87-078-1 (paperback)
Mandarin, 1991, 1992 (U.K.) ISBN 0-7493-1170-3 (paperback) (entitled *Monty Python's Papperbok*)

MONTY PYTHON AND THE HOLY GRAIL (BOOK) (has also been cited as **MONTY PYTHON'S SECOND FILM: A FIRST DRAFT and MØNTI PYTHØN IK DEN HØLIE GRÄILEN (BØK)),** by Graham Chapman, John Cleese, Terry Gilliam, Eric Idle, Terry Jones, and Michael Palin (contains the first draft, final draft, production notes, sketches, and both production and candid photos, and is packaged to look like an actual script)

Eyre Methuen Ltd., 1977 (reprinted in 1979 and 1981) (U.K.) ISBN 0-413-38520-5 (paperback)
Methuen Inc., 1977 (U.S.) ISBN 0-416-00341-9
Methuen Publications, 1977 (Canada) ISBN 0-458-92970-0 (paperback) (features a plain black die-cut cover)
Mandarin Paperbacks / Michelin House, 1992, 1993 (U.K.) ISBN 0-7493-1142-8 (paperback)

MONTY PYTHON THE LIFE OF BRIAN / MONTYPYTHONSCRAP-BOOK (has also been cited as **MONTY PYTHON'S THE LIFE OF BRIAN (OF NAZARETH)** and **MONTYPYTHONSCRAPBOOKOFBRIANOF-NAZARETH**), by Graham Chapman, John Cleese, Terry Gilliam, Eric Idle, Terry Jones, and Michael Palin (one half of the book contains the final script of the film, illustrated with photos from the movie; the other half is printed upside-down and contains a random assortment of Python material, some of it related to the film; includes lyrics to the "Philosopher's Song")

Methuen, 1979 (U.K.) ISBN 0-413-46550-0 (oversized trade paperback)
Fred Jordan Books / Grosset & Dunlap, 1979 (U.S.) ISBN 0-448-16568-6 (also cited as ISBN 0-4418-568-6) (oversized trade paperback)
Mandarin, 1991 (U.K.) ISBN 0-7493-0997-0 (oversized trade paperback)

MONTY PYTHON'S LIFE OF BRIAN, by Graham Chapman, John Cleese, Terry Gilliam, Eric Idle, Terry Jones, and Michael Palin
(small paperback version of the script originally printed in the oversized edition, including all of the photographs, but without any of the scrapbook material)

Ace Books, 1979 (U.S.) ISBN 0-441-48240-6 (paperback)

THE CONTRACTUAL OBLIGATION SONGBOOK, by Graham Chapman, John Cleese, Terry Gilliam, Eric Idle, Terry Jones, and Michael Palin

EMI Music Academy, 1980 (U.K.) I

THE COMPLETE WORKS OF SHAKESPEARE AND MONTY PYTHON: VOLUME ONE - MONTY PYTHON, by Graham Chapman, John Cleese, Terry Gilliam, Eric Idle, Terry Jones, and Michael Palin (British compilation of *Big Red Book* and *Brand New Monty Python Bok*; cover shows bookshelf of several very worn volumes, presumably Shakespeare, and the two Monty Python books)

Book Club Associates, 1981 (U.K.) ISBN 0-413-49450-0 (hardcover)

MONTY PYTHON'S THE MEANING OF LIFE, by Graham Chapman, John Cleese, Terry Gilliam, Eric Idle, Terry Jones, and Michael Palin (script of the film, complete with color illustrations and many photographs from the film; includes segments removed from the final print of the film such as *The Adventures of Martin Luther*, also includes many photographs from the Terry Gilliam short film *The Crimson Permanent Assurance*)

Methuen, 1983 (U.K.) ISBN 0-413-53380-8 (paperback)
Grove Press, 1983 (U.S.) ISBN 0-394-62474-2 (***)
Mandarin, 1991 (U.K.) ISBN 0-7493-1223-8 (***)

THE GOLDEN SKITS OF WING COMMANDER MURIEL VOLESTRANGLER FRHS & BAR (1984) (includes text to a number of Monty Python sketches; see John Cleese)

THE MONTY PYTHON GIFT BOKS, by Graham Chapman, John Cleese, Terry Gilliam, Eric Idle, Terry Jones, and Michael Palin (repackaging of the *Monty Python's Big Red Book* and *The Brand New Monty Python Papperbok*, with an additional poster)

Methuen, 1986, 1988, ISBN 0-413-14520-4 (paperback)

MONTY PYTHON'S FLYING CIRCUS: JUST THE WORDS, VOLUME ONE, by Graham Chapman, John Cleese, Terry Gilliam, Eric Idle, Terry Jones, and Michael Palin (complete scripts of the Flying Circus television series, volume one includes episodes 1 through 23; includes an index and a listing of production and airing dates)

Methuen, 1989 (U.K.) ISBN 0-413-62540-0 (hardcover)
Pantheon, 1989 (U.S.) ISBN 0-679-72647-0 (paperback) (U.S. version titled *The Complete Monty Python's Flying Circus: All The Words, Volume One*)
Haffmans Verlag AG Zürich, 1993 (Germany) ISBN 3-453-09235-X (paperback) (German version titled *Monty Python's Flying Circus: Samtliche Worte, Band Eins*)

MONTY PYTHON'S FLYING CIRCUS: JUST THE WORDS, VOLUME TWO, by Graham Chapman, John Cleese, Terry Gilliam, Eric Idle,

Terry Jones, and Michael Palin (complete scripts of the Flying Circus television series, volume two includes episodes 24 through 45; includes an index and a listing of production and airing dates)

Methuen London, Ltd., 1989 (U.K.) ISBN 0-413-62550-8 (hardcover)
Pantheon, 1989 (U.S.) ISBN 0-679-72648-9 (paperback) (U.S. version titled *The Complete Monty Python's Flying Circus: All The Words, Volume Two*)

Haffmans Verlag AG Zürich, 1993 (Germany) (paperback) (German version titled *Monty Python's Flying Circus: Samtliche Worte, Band Zwei*; entirely in German)

MONTY PYTHON'S FLYING CIRCUS: JUST THE WORDS (has also been cited as **THE COMPLETE MONTY PYTHON**), by Graham Chapman, John Cleese, Terry Gilliam, Eric Idle, Terry Jones, and Michael Palin (volumes one and two combined together into one regular size paperback; volume two is printed upside-down; includes two sections of photographs from the television series)

Methuen / Mandarin, 1990, 1992, 1993, 1994 (U.K.) ISBN 0-7493-0226-7 (paperback)

MONTY PYTHON DAS LEBEN BRIANS, aus dem Englischen von Michael Bodmer (script text of *Monty Python's Life of Brian* film entirely in German; includes text for omitted scenes and black and white photos from the film)

Haffmans Verlag AG Zürich, 1992 (Germany) ISBN 3-251-30036-9 (hardcover)

MONTY PYTHON DER SINN DES LEBENS, aus dem Englischen von Bernd Eilert (complete script of *Monty Python's The Meaning of Life*, but entirely in German; includes text for all of the songs in the film in English)

Haffmans Verlag AG Zürich, 1993 (Germany) ISBN 3-251-30024-5 (hardcover)

THE FAIRLY INCOMPLETE & RATHER BADLY ILLUSTRATED MONTY PYTHON SONG BOOK, by Graham Chapman, John Cleese, Terry Gilliam, Eric Idle, Terry Jones, and Michael Palin (includes lyrics and voice scores to virtually all of the Monty Python songs, such as the "Lumberjack Song" (including the Holzfaeller version from the German episodes), the "Spam Song", the "Philosopher's Song", and "Always Look on the Bright Side of Life"; it is illustrated with Terry Gilliam's artwork and a collection of photographs from the television series and movies)

Methuen London, Ltd., 1994 (U.K.) ISBN 0-413-69000-8 (hardcover) (comes with free CD single which includes the "Spam Song" and the "Lumberjack Song")
Harper Perennial, 1995 (U.S.) ISBN 0-06-095116-8 (paperback)

FREMDSPRACHENTEXTE: MONTY PYTHON'S FLYING CIRCUS: SELECTED SKETCHES, Herausgegeben von Reinhard Gratzke (small German textbook for learning English as a foreign language; uses Monty Python sketches to teach English terms and phrases; includes complete text for Flying Circus Series 1, Episode 1; Series 2, Episode 8; Series 3, Episode 11; as well as selected sketches including "Nudge, Nudge (na!, na!)", "Dead Parrot", and "Argument Clinic")

Philipp Reclam jun. GmbH & Co., 1995 (Germany) ISBN 3-15-009023-7 (paperback)

MONTY PYTHON: DIE NACKTE AMEISE, Deutsch von Christian Storms (a very small book in the Heyne Mini series, titled *Monty Python; The Naked Ant*; features all of the sketches from episode twelve of *Monty Python's Flying Circus* in German; these small booklets are purchased ten at a time)

Wilhelm Heyne Verlag GmbH & Co. KG, 1996 (Germany) ISBN 3-453-09510-3 (paperback)

AUDIO RECORDINGS

LP = Long Playing Record Album; SI = Single; CS = Cassette Tape; CD = Compact Disc

A.MONTY PYTHON
MONTY PYTHON'S FLYING CIRCUS (1970)

SIDE ONE: Flying Sheep / Television Interviews / Arthur Frampton / Trade Description Act / Whizzo Chocolates / Nudge, Nudge; The Mouse Problem / Buying A Bed / Interesting People / The Barber / Lumberjack Song; Interviews / Sir Edward Ross

SIDE TWO: More Television Interviews / Arthur / "Two Sheds" Jackson / Children's Stories / The Visitors / The Cinema / Albatross / The North Minehead By-Election / Me Doctor / Pet Shop (Dead Parrot) / Self-Defense

LP: (1970) BBC Records REB 73M (U.K.)
LP: (1970) Pye Records 12116 (U.S.) (features a slightly different back-cover than the original BBC version)
LP: (1970) BBC Records BBC-22073 (U.K.)
CS: (1970) BBC Records REMC 73 (U.K.)

CD: (1985) BBC / Audio Visual International BBC CD 73 (U.K.)

LP: (1986) Warner Brothers Records 88375 (ISBN 0-871-88375-9) (U.S.)

CS: (1994) BBC Enterprises, Ltd. ZBBC 1508 ISBN 0-563-39481-1 (U.K.) (Canned Laughter series)

CD: (1997) DerHörVerlag / Originalton CD 1 ISBN 3-89584-509-4 (Germany) (German reissue, with introduction in German)

ANOTHER MONTY PYTHON RECORD (1971)

(packaged as "Beethoven Symphony No. 2 In D Major" and defaced by the Pythons to serve as their own record jacket. Most of the material is re-recorded versions of TV sketches, although some have been altered slightly; there are also a few new sketches and new linking material)

SIDE ONE: Apologies / Spanish Inquisition / World Forum / Gumby Theatre, Etc. / The Architect / The Piranha Brothers

SIDE TWO: Death Of Mary, Queen Of Scots / Penguin On The TV / Comfy Chair / Sound Quiz / Be A Great Actor / Theatre Quiz / Royal Festival Hall Concert / Spam / The Judges / Stake Your Claim / Still No Sign Of Land / Undertaker

LP: (1970) Charisma Records Ltd., CAS 1049 (U.K.)

LP: (1972) Charisma CAS 1049 (U.S.) (with different running-order and material)

LP: (1972) Buddah, (U.S.)

LP: (1988) Virgin Records Ltd., CHC 79 (U.K.) (budget price)

LP: (19***) Virgin MP501 (U.K.)

CD: (1989) Virgin Records Ltd. CASCD 1049 ("Another Monty Python CD") (U.S.)

CD: (1994) Virgin Records, Ltd., VCCD 001 (U.K.) ("Another Monty Python CD" version 2, re-issue)

MONTY PYTHON'S PREVIOUS RECORD (1972)

(contains a mixture of material from the TV shows, largely the third series, as well as new material. "A Fairy Tale" is a shortened version of a sketch done by John Cleese and Connie Booth for one of the German Python shows; some versions of this record came with the "Teach Yourself Heath" flexidisc)

SIDE ONE: Embarrassment / A Bed-Time Book / England 1747—Dennis Moore / Money Programme / Dennis Moore Continues / Australian Table Wines / Argument Clinic / Putting Budgies Down / Eric The Half A Bee / Travel Agency

SIDE TWO: Radio Quiz Game; / A Massage / City Noises Quiz; Miss Anne Elk / We Love The Yangtse / How-To-Do-It Lessons / A Minute Passed / Eclipse Of The Sun / Alistair Cooke / Wonderful World Of Sounds / A Fairy Tale

LP: (1972) Charisma, CAS 1063 (U.K.)
LP: (1972) Charisma (has also been cited as Arista), 0598 (U.S.)
LP: (1973) Buddah, (U.S.)
LP: (19***) Virgin MP506 (U.K.)
LP: (1988) Virgin Records Ltd., CHC 80 (U.K.) (budget price)
CD: (1989) Virgin Records Ltd., CASCD 1063 (U.K.) (budget CD)
CD: (1994) Virgin Records Ltd., VCCD 002 (U.K.) (reissue)

THE MONTY PYTHON MATCHING TIE AND HANDKERCHIEF (1973)

(some LP versions of this recording include the infamous third side; the second side of the album actually has two separate grooves with entirely different material recorded on them; listeners will hear either track depending on where the record needle is placed; subsequent pressings did not include the third side)

SIDE ONE: Dead Bishop on the Landing / The Church Police / Who Cares / The Surgeon and the Elephant Mr. Humphries / Thomas Hardy / Novel Writing / Word Association; Bruces / Philosophers' Song / Nothing Happened / Eating Dog; Cheese Shop / Thomas Hardy / Tiger Club / Great Actors

SIDE TWO: Infant Minister for Overseas Development / Oscar Wilde's Party / Pet Shop Conversions / Mr. Phone-in

SIDE THREE: Background To History / Medieval / Open Field Farming

Songs / World War I Soldier / Stuck Record / Boxing Tonight With Kenneth Clark

LP: (1973) Charisma CAS 1080 (U.K.) (sleeve is drawn and shaped like a box with a square cut-out window; a matching tie and handkerchief is visible through the window. The tie and handkerchief are actually attached to a gruesome character hanging from a gallows and is depicted on a separate sheet which one can pull out; there is also a separate green colored insert with silly information about the record and "The Background to History")

LP: (1985) Charisma CAS 1080 (U.K.) (this reprint of the original album has a perfectly square sleeve with basically the same design except that there is no window, the tie and handkerchief are part of the cover art; there are no inserts)

LP: (1975) Arista AL 4039 (U.S.) (features a different design on the cover than the U.K. Charisma LP; the window is oval rather than square and the gruesome character and "The Background to History" inserts actually make up the inner sleeve)

LP: (1975) Arista ALB 4039 (U.S.) (single groove censored banded promo)

LP: Virgin MP505 (U.K.)

LP: Arista ALB 68357 (U.S.)

LP: (1988) Virgin Records Ltd., CHC 81 (U.K.) (budget price; single groove on side B)

CS: Arista ACB6-8357 (U.S.)

CD: (1985, 1989) Virgin Records Ltd. CASCD 1080 (U.K.) (budget CD)

CD: Arista / BMG 07822-18357-2 (Canada) (features same cover as U.S. Arista LP)

CD: (1994) Virgin Records Ltd., VCCD 003 (U.K.) (reissue)

CD: (1997) Arista / Arista Masters 07822-18956-2 (U.S.) (part of The Monty Python Masters re-release series by Arista)

MONTY PYTHON LIVE AT THE THEATRE ROYAL, DRURY LANE (1974)

(recorded during the Pythons' live stage performances at the Theatre Royal, Drury Lane; the Pythons performed at Drury Lane from February through March 1974)

SIDE ONE: Introduction / Llamas; Gumby Flower Arranging / Secret Service; Wrestling / Communist Quiz / Idiot Song (Neil Innes) / Albatross / The Colonel / Nudge, Nudge / Cocktail Bar / Travel Agent

SIDE TWO: Spot The Brain Cell / Bruces; Argument / Four Yorkshiremen / Election Special / Lumberjack Song; Parrot

LP: (1974, 1983) Charisma Records, Ltd. / Charisma, Class 4 (U.K.)
LP: Charisma Records, CAS 1141 (U.S.)
LP: Virgin MP504 (U.K.) (catalog number is questionable)
LP: (1989) VIP Records, VVIP 104 (U.K.) (budget price)
CS: Virgin Records Ltd. CA4-1-1502 (Canada) (*Monty Python Live at Drury Lane*)
CD: (1989) VIP Records, VVIPD 104 (U.K.) (budget CD)
CD: Virgin / EMI / Axis CDVAX 701612 (Australia) (*Monty Python Live at Drury Lane*)
CD: (1994) Virgin Records Ltd., VCCD 007 (U.K.) (*Monty Python Live at Drury Lane;* reissue)

THE ALBUM OF THE SOUNDTRACK OF THE TRAILER OF THE FILM OF MONTY PYTHON AND THE HOLY GRAIL (1975)

(contains excerpts from the film soundtrack, plus other film related linking material)

SIDE ONE: Congratulations / Welcome To The Cinema / Opening / Coconuts / Bring Out Your Dead / King Arthur Meets Dennis / Class Struggle / Witch Test / Professional Logician; Camelot / The Quest / The Silbury Hill Car Park / Frenchmen Of The Castle / Bomb Threat / Executive Announcement

SIDE TWO: Story Of The Film So Far / The Tale Of Sir Robin / The Knights Of Ni / Interview / Director Carl French / Swamp Castle / The Guards / Tim / The Enchanter / Great Performances / Angry Crowd / Holy Hand Grenade / Announcement—Sir Kenneth Clark / French Castle Again / Close

LP: (1975) Charisma CAS 1103 (U.K.)
LP: (1983) Charisma CHC 17 (U.K.) (special reissue at budget price)
LP: Arista AL 4050 (U.S.)
LP: Virgin MP503 (U.K.)
LP: Arista Al 5-8157 (U.S.)
LP: Arista ALB 68355 (U.S.)
CS: (1975) Arista Records Inc. ACB6-8355 (U.S.)
CD: (1989) Virgin CASCD1103 (U.K.) (budget CD)
CD: (1994) Virgin Records Ltd., VCCD 004 (U.K.) (reissue)

CD: (1997) Arista / Arista Masters 07822-18958-2 (U.S.) (part of *The Monty Python Masters* re-release series by Arista)

THE WORST BEST... MONTY PYTHON (has also been cited as THE WORST OF MONTY PYTHON and THE WORST / BEST OF MONTY PYTHON) (1976)

(title actually reads "The Worst Best... Monty Python" with the word "Worst" crossed out; this is actually a repackaging of *Another Monty Python Record* (CAS 1049) and *Monty Python's Previous Record* (CAS 1063) a gatefold sleeve and a new album jacket that features Gilliamesque artwork by another artist (Jim O'Connell); features a transposed running-order on disc one)

SIDE ONE: Apologies / Spanish Inquisition / World Forum / Gumby Theatre / The Architect / The Piranha Brothers

SIDE TWO: Death of Mary Queen of Scots / Penguin on the T.V. / Comfy Chair / Sound Quiz / Be a Great Actor / Theatre Critic / Royal Festival Hall Concert / SPAM / The Judges / Stake Your Claim / Still No Sign of Land / The Undertaker

SIDE THREE: Embarrassment / A Bed Time Book / England 1747 - Dennis Moore / Money Programme / Dennis Moore Continues / Australian Table Wines / Argument Clinic / Putting Down Budgies and So Forth; Eric the Half a Bee / Travel Agency

SIDE FOUR: Radio Quiz Game / A Massage / City Noises Quiz / Miss Anne Elk / We Love the Yangtse / How-to-Do-It Lessons / A Minute Passed / Eclipse of the Sun / Alastaire Cooke; Wonderful World of Sounds / A Fairy Tale

LP: (1974) Buddah Records, BDS 5656-2 (U.S.) (some copies of the album were incorrectly labeled as 5626-2 and had sides A and B incorrectly labeled)

MONTY PYTHON'S PREVIOUS RECORD / ANOTHER MONTY PYTHON RECORD (1976)

(Same as *"The Worst of Monty Python,"* which is a repackaging of *"Another Monty Python Record"* and *"Monty Python's Previous Record"* it comes as a double-album set with their original covers)

LP: (1976) *Kama Sutra* KSBS2611-2 (U.S.)

MONTY PYTHON LIVE AT CITY CENTER (1976)

(recorded live at New York's City Center, where the Pythons performed their live show for three weeks (April 14-May 2, 1976); this album is based on the first few performances so that Arista could release the album in stores before the show closed; this album was not released on compact disc until 1997)

SIDE ONE: Introduction / Llama / Gumby Flower Arranging / Short Blues (Neil Innes) / Wrestling / World Forum / Albatross / Colonel Stopping It / Nudge, Nudge / Crunchy Frog; Bruces Song / Travel Agent

SIDE TWO: Camp Judges / Blackmail / Protest Song (Neil Innes) / Pet Shop / Four Yorkshiremen / Argument Clinic / Death Of Mary, Queen Of Scots / Salvation Fuzz / Church Police / Lumberjack Song

LP: (1976) Arista AL 4073 (U.S.) (*"Monty Python Live! At City Center"*)
LP: (1976) Arista ALB 4073 (U.S.) (*"Monty Python Live! At City Center;"* censored banded promo)
LP: (1976) Kay Gee Bee Songs, Inc., AB 4073 (***)
LP: (1976) Arista ALB6-8353 (U.S.)
CS: (1976) Arista Records Inc., ACB6-8353 (U.S.)
CD: (1997) Arista / Arista Masters 07822-18957-2 (U.S.) (part of *The Monty Python Masters* re-release series by Arista)

THE MONTY PYTHON INSTANT RECORD COLLECTION, THE PICK OF THE BEST OF SOME RECENTLY REPEATED PYTHON HITS AGAIN, VOL. II (1977)

(originally designed by Terry Gilliam and packaged to fold out into a cardboard box resembling a large stack of record albums, and now released in a normal record sleeve because the package kept breaking open in stores, this is essentially a greatest hits album, or, as it is billed, "The pick of the best of some recently repeated Python hits again, Vol. II." Most of the material here has been on previous albums)

SIDE ONE: Introductions / Alistair Cooke / Nudge, Nudge / Mrs. Nigger-Baiter / Constitutional Peasants / Fish License / Eric The Half A Bee / Australian Table Wines / Silly Noises; Novel Writing / Elephantoplasty / How To Do It / Gumby Cherry Orchard / Oscar Wilde

SIDE TWO: Introduction / Argument / French Taunter / Summarize Proust Competition / Cheese Emporium / Funerals At Prestatyn / Camelot / Word Association / Bruces / Parrot / Monty Python Theme

LP: (1977, 1983) Charisma CAS 1134 (U.K.)
LP: (1977) Charisma / GRT CAS 1134 (9211-1134) (Canada)
LP: (1981) Arista Records ALB6-8296 (U.S.)
CD: (1989) Virgin Records, Ltd., CASCD 1134 (U.K.) (budget CD)

THE MONTY PYTHON INSTANT RECORD COLLECTION, THE PICK OF THE BEST OF SOME RECENTLY REPEATED PYTHON HITS AGAIN, VOL. II (1977)

(different collection of best hits than the original U.K. version, features tracks from *"Matching Tie and Handkerchief," "The Album . . . Holy Grail," "Live at City Center,"* and *"Contractual Obligation Album"*)

SIDE ONE: The Executive Intro / Pet Shop / Nudge, Nudge / Live

Broadcast from London / Premiere of Film / Bring Out Your Dead / How Do You Tell A Witch / Camelot / Argument Clinic / Crunchy Frog / The Cheese Shop / The Phone-In / Sit On My Face

SIDE TWO: Another Executive Announcement / Bishop On The Landing / Elephantoplasty / The Lumberjack Song / Bookshop / Blackmail / Farewell to John Denver / World Forum / String / Wide World of Novel Writing / Death of Mary, Queen of Scots / Never Be Rude to an Arab

LP: (1981) Arista Records AL 9580 (U.S.)
CS: (1982) Arista Records Inc. ACB6-8296 (U.S.)
CD: (1990) Arista ARCD-8296 (U.S.) (features different cover from Arista cassette)

MONTY PYTHON'S LIFE OF BRIAN (1979)
(contains excerpts from the film, with brief linking material by Eric idle and Graham Chapman)

SIDE ONE: Introduction / Three Wise Men / Brian Song / Big Nose / The Stoning / Ex-Leper / Bloody Romans / Link / People's Front Of Judea / Short Link / Latin Lesson / Missing Link / Revolutionary Meeting / Very Good Link / Ben / Audience With Pilate / Meanwhile

SIDE TWO: The Prophets / Haggling / Lobster / Sermon On The Wall / Lobster Link / Simon The Holy Man / Sex Link / The Morning After / Lighter Link / Pilate And Biggus / Welease Bwian / Nisus Wettus / Crucifixion / Always Look On The Bright Side Of Life / Close

LP: (1979) Warner Brothers K 56751 (U.K.)
LP: (1979) Warner Brothers BSK 3396 (U.S.)
CS: (1979) Warner Bros. K 456751 (U.K.)
CD: (1994) Virgin Chattering Classics VCCD 009 (U.K.)

THE WARNER BROTHERS MUSIC SHOW: MONTY PYTHON EXAMINES "THE LIFE OF BRIAN" (1979)

(a promotional album released to radio stations as part of the Warners series and never sold. It consists of an hour-long interview with the Pythons conducted by Dave Herman, along with excerpts from the soundtrack, a Monumental Blunders Production)

LP: (1979) WBMS 110 (U.S.)

MONTY PYTHON'S CONTRACTUAL OBLIGATION ALBUM (1980)

(this record contains all-new material, except for "String" and "Bookshop", both of which predate Python. "Farewell to John Denver" was deleted from later pressings for legal reasons, while "Sit on My Face", reportedly faced legal threats, as it is sung to the tune of "Sing As We Go", an old Gracie Fields tune. This is easily the most musical of any Python album, with over half of the twenty-four tracks consisting of songs)

SIDE ONE: Sit On My Face / Announcement / Henry Kissinger; String / Never Be Rude To An Arab / I Like Chinese / Bishop / Medical Love Song / Farewell To John Denver / Finland / I'm So Worried

SIDE TWO: I Bet You They Won't Play This Song On The Radio / Martyrdom Of St. Victor / Here Comes Another One / Bookshop / Do What John / Rock Notes / Muddy Knees / Crocodile / Decomposing Composers / Bells / Traffic Lights / All Things Dull And Ugly / A Scottish Farewell

LP: (1980) Charisma CAS 1152 (U.K.) (features sleeve jacket with handwritten notes by the Pythons and makes reference to the John Denver song; released October 1980)
LP: (1980) Charisma CAS 1152 (U.K.) (does not include the "Farewell to John Denver" song; released November 1980)
LP: (1980) Charisma CHC 34 (U.K.) (censored, budget price)
LP: (1980 Arista AL 9536 (U.S.) (features sleeve jacket with handwritten notes by the Pythons; record itself features labels which appear scratched up with handwritten "Side One" and "The Other Side" on them)

LP: (1980) Arista ALDJ 9536 (U.S.) (promotional copy of the U.S. release of the album; features plain white cover with track listing on the back; record itself is just labeled "Monty Python" with track listings on them)

LP: Virgin MP502 (U.K.)

LP: (1980) Arista ALB6-8343 (U.S.)

CS: (1980) Arista ACB6-8343 (U.S.) (cover features image of old cassette tape with the title covered with white liquid paper and "Monty Python's Contractual O..." written across it in the same fashion of the original LP cover)

CD: (1989) Virgin Records Ltd. / Kay Gee Be Music Ltd. CASCD 1152 (U.K.) (budget CD)

CD: (1994) Virgin Records Ltd., VCCD 008 (U.K.) (censored version; reissue)

CD: (1994) Arista Records / BMG, 0-7822-18343-2 (Canada) (includes some additional written text on the cover)

CD: (1997) Arista / Arista Masters 07822-18955-2 (U.S.) (part of *The Monty Python Masters* re-release series by Arista)

MONTY PYTHON'S CONTRACTUAL OBLIGATION SAMPLER (1980)

(white cover with center hole; album sticker says "Side One: all-purpose, okey-dokey, non-offensive side for radio, stores, parties and christenings. Side Two: hilariously funny yet NASTY side on which Pythons sling racial invective and name bodily parts. NOT FOR AIRPLAY")

SIDE ONE: I Bet You They Won't Play This Song on the Radio / I like Chinese / Farewell to John Denver / Rock Notes / Decomposing Composers / Sit on my Face.

SIDE TWO: Henry Kissinger / Never Be Rude to an Arab / Medical Love Song / All Things Dull and Ugly / Crocodile

LP: (1980) Arista SP 101 (U.S.)

ALL THE WORST OF MONTY PYTHON (1981)

(six LP set of *"Another Monty Python Record"* (CAS 1049), *"Monty Python's Previous Record"* (CAS 1063), *"The Monty Python Matching Tie and Handkerchief"* (CAS 1080), *"Monty Python Live at Drury Lane"* (CLASS 4), *"The Album of the Soundtrack of the Trailer of the Film of Monty Python and the Holy Grail"* (CAS

1103), and *"Monty Python's Contractual Obligation Album"* (CAS 1152))

LP: (1981) Charisma 6685 081 (Australia)

MONTY PYTHON'S THE MEANING OF LIFE (1983)
(contains excerpts from the film, with new linking material)

SIDE ONE: Introduction / Fish Introduction / The Meaning Of Life / Birth; Birth Link / Frying Eggs / Every Sperm Is Sacred / Protestant Couple / Adventures Of Martin Luther / Sex Education / Trench Warfare / The Great Tea Of 1914-18 / Fish Link

SIDE TWO: Terry Gilliam's Intro / Accountancy Shanty / Theme Zulu Wars / Link / The Dungeon Restaurant / Link / Live Organ Transplants / The Galaxy Song / The Not Noel Coward (Penis) Song / Mr. Creosote / The Grim Reaper / Christmas In Heaven / Dedication (To Fish)

LP: (1983) MCA Records MCA 6121 (***)
LP: (1983) CBS Inc. CBS 70239 (U.K.)
CS: (1983) MCA Records MCAC-6121 (***)
CD: (1994) Virgin Chattering Classics VCCD 010 (U.K.)

THE MEANING OF LIFE AUDIO PRESS KIT
(Box set with trailers and interview LPs, plus press kit)

LP: (1983) Universal City Studios (U.S.)

MONTY PYTHON'S THE FINAL RIP OFF (1988)
(another "greatest hits" compilation. released when Virgin took over the Monty Python catalogue. This represents their first double-record set. All material here has been performed on previous records, except for some brief links by Michael Palin)

SIDE ONE: Introduction / Constitutional Peasants / Fish License / Eric The Half A Bee / Finland Song / Travel Agent / Are You Embarrassed Easily? / Australian Table Wines / Argument / Henry Kissinger Song / Parrot (Oh, Not Again !)

SIDE TWO: Sit On My Face / Undertaker / Novel Writing (Live From Wessex) / String / Bells; Traffic Lights / Cocktail Bar / Four Yorkshiremen / Election Special / Lumberjack Song

SIDE THREE: I Like Chinese / Spanish Inquisition Part 1 / Cheese Shop / Cherry Orchard / Architects' Sketch / Spanish Inquisition Part 2 / Spam / Spanish Inquisition Part 3 / Comfy Chair / Famous Person Quiz / You Be The Actor / Nudge, Nudge / Cannibalism / Spanish Inquisition Revisited

SIDE FOUR: I Bet You They Won't Play This Song On The Radio / Bruces; Bookshop / Do Wot John / Rock Notes / I'm So Worried / Crocodile / French Taunter Part 1 / Marilyn Monroe / Swamp Castle / French Taunter Part 2 / Last Word

LP: (1988) Virgin Records Virgin 7 90865-1 (U.S.)
LP: (1987) Virgin Records Ltd., MPD 1 (U.K.) (gatefold sleeve)
CS: (1988) Virgin Records Ltd., 7 90865-4 (U.S.)
CD: (1987) Virgin Records CDMP 1 (U.K.) (many of these were mistakenly packaged with two copies of the same disc, rather than containing a disc 1 and a disc 2)
CD: (1987) Virgin Records 7 86033 2 0 (U.S.)
CD: Virgin Records 7 90865 2 (***)

MONTY PYTHON SINGS (1989)

(a collection of almost all of the Monty Python songs; includes a previously unreleased track, "Oliver Cromwell;" released with libretto 1989; repromoted in 1991)

TRACK LISTING: Always Look on the Bright Side of Life / Sit on My Face / Lumberjack Song / Penis Song (Not the Noel Coward Song) / Oliver Cromwell / Money Song / Accountancy Shanty / Finland / Medical Love Song / I'm So Worried / Every Sperm is Sacred / Never Be Rude to an Arab / I Like Chinese / Eric the Half a Bee / Brian Song / Bruces' Philosophers Song (Bruces' Song) / Meaning of Life / Knights of the Round Table / All Things Dull and Ugly / Decomposing Composers / Henry Kissinger / I've Got Two Legs / Christmas in Heaven / Galaxy Song / Spam Song

CS: (1989) Virgin Records Ltd., MONT 1 (U.K.)
CS: (1989) Virgin Records Ltd., MONTC 1 Virgin 25 (U.K)
CS: Virgin Records 91781-4 (***)
CD: Virgin Records 91781-2 (***)
CD: (1989) Virgin Records / Kay Gee Bee Music Ltd. CDV 3133 (U.S.)
CD: (1989, 1991) Virgin Records, Ltd., MONTD 1 (U.K.) (with libretto; repromoted in 1991)

THE ULTIMATE MONTY PYTHON RIP OFF (1994)

(another collection of previously recorded skits, released in U.K.; more of a promotional album for *"The Instant Monty Python CD Collection"*)

TRACK LISTING: Introduction / Finland / Travel Agent / I Like Chinese / French Taunter / Australian Table Wines / Spanish Inquisition / The Galaxy Song / Every Sperm is Sacred / Grim Reaper / Sit on My Face / Argument / Mary Queen of Scots / Four Yorkshiremen / Lumberjack Song /

Albatross / Nudge, Nudge / Parrot / Bruces / Philosophers' Song / Fish License / Eric the Half-a-Bee / The Spam Song / Big Nose / Stoning / Link I / Welease Wodger / Link 2 / Always Look on the Bright Side of Life / Spanish Inquisition (Ending)

CD: (1994) Virgin Records, Ltd. / Kay Gee Bee Music Ltd. CDV 2748 (U.K.)

THE INSTANT MONTY PYTHON CD COLLECTION (1994)
(six CD volume set; includes "Another Monty Python Record," "Monty Python's Previous Record," "Matching Tie and Handkerchief," "Live at Drury Lane," "Monty Python and the Holy Grail," "Contractual Obligation Album," "Life of Brian," and "Meaning of Life;" also includes 40 page booklet)

CS: (1994) Virgin Records, Ltd.
CD: (1994) Virgin Records, Ltd., CDBOX 3, ISBN 1-885381-04-2 (U.S.)

THE MONTY PYTHON CD SAMPLER THINGY: LUST FOR GLORY (1995)
(U.S. promotional CD for "The Instant Monty Python CD Collection;" cover art is an original Terry Gilliam piece designed for the 25th anniversary Monty Python Lust for Glory! Festival; tracks are taken from the "Another Monty Python Record," "Monty Python's Previous Record," "Live at Drury Lane," and "Life of Brian;" some of the tracks have been edited for length and content; obscenities were removed)

TRACK LISTING: Liberty Bell / Spanish Inquisition Part 1 / Spanish Inquisition Part 2 / Spanish Inquisition / The Comfy Chair / Theatre Critic / Royal Festival Hall Concert / Spam / Spam Song / The Judges / Embarrassment / A Bed Time Book / England 1747 - Dennis Moore / Money Programme / The Money Song / Australian Wines / How To Do It / Fish License / Eric The Half A Bee / Radio

Quiz Game / City [sic] Noises Quiz / Communist Quiz / Nudge, Nudge / Four Yorkshiremen / Lumberjack Song / Parrot Sketch / Introduction / Three Wise Men / Brian Song / Peoples Front of Judea / Always Look on the Bright Side of Life

CD: (1995) Virgin Records, DPRO-14236 (U.S.)

B.MONTY PYTHON (THE SINGLES)
FLYING SHEEP / A MAN WITH THREE BUTTOCKS (1970)
(presumably a single from the original "Flying Circus" album; existence unconfirmed)

SI:(1970) BBC, (U.K.)

THE LEAST BIZARRE OF MONTY PYTHON (1971, has also been cited as 1972)
(six track promo album which was a sampler of "Another Monty Python Record" (CAS 1049))

SI:(1971) Charisma, CMP-EP (U.S.)

THE LUMBERJACK SONG / SPAM SONG (1971)

SI:(1971, 1974, 1975) Charisma CB 268 (not sure about release year, November 14, 1975?)

ERIC THE HALF A BEE / YANGTSE SONG (has also been cited as ERIC THE HALF A BEE / ERIC THE HALF A BEE) (1972)
(has been cited as a 7-inch double-A-sided single as well as a regular A & B-sided single)

SI:(1972) Charisma CB 200 (U.K.)

SPAM SONG / THE CONCERT (1972)

SI:(1972) Charisma CB 192

TEACH YOURSELF HEATH (1972)

(flexidisc included free in the inner sleeve of some versions of "Monty Python's Previous Record" as well as the December 1972 rock magazine "ZigZag;" includes original material with an introduction by Michael Palin, lesson by Eric Idle, and examples by Edward Heath)

SI:(1972) Python Productions / Zig Zag, December 1972 (U.K.)

MONTY PYTHON'S TINY BLACK ROUND THING (has also been cited as MONTY PYTHON'S TINY BLACK ROUND THING - D.P. GUMBY PRESENTS "ELECTION '74" / LUMBERJACK SONG (RECORDED LIVE NEAR ALF'S CAFF, DRURY LANE)) (1974)

(Election '74 / Lumberjack Song taken from the *"Drury Lane"* album included free with British rock magazine *"New Musical Express"* (May 1974); it includes new intro by Michael Palin as D.P. Gumby)

SI:(1974) New Musical Express / Charisma Sound For Industry, Charisma SO 1259 (has also been cited as SFI 1259) (U.K.) (has also been cited as being released in 1977)

THE SINGLE (1975)

(this is a promotional single for the "Matching Tie and Handkerchief" album, containing shortened versions of: Who Cares / The Elephant Mr. Humphries; Infant Minister for Overseas Development; Pet Shop Conversions)

SI:(1975) Arista ASDJ 0103 (has also been cited as AS 0103) (U.S.)

PYTHON ON SONG (1976)

(a two-record set released in the U.K.; includes the "Lumberjack Song / Spam Song" single (Charisma CB 268) and the "Eric the Half a Bee / Bruce's Live At Drury Lane" single (PY2); double pack, gatefold sleeve, some versions came with seal and were signed)

RECORD 1, Side A: Lumberjack Song (Produced by George Harrison); Side B: Spam Song

RECORD 2, Side A: Bruces Song (with Neil Innes, from Drury Lane);
Side B: Eric the Half a Bee

SI:(1976) Charisma MP 001 (U.K.)

ALWAYS LOOK ON THE BRIGHT SIDE OF LIFE / BRIAN SONG (1978)
(A-side credited to "Sonia Jones")

SI:(1978) Warner Brothers K 17495 (U.K.)
SI:(1978) Warner Brothers K 17495 PRO (U.S.) (7-inch promo single; censored B-side)

I LIKE CHINESE / I'LL BET YOU THEY WON'T PLAY THIS SONG ON THE RADIO / FINLAND (1980)
(songs from *Monty Python's Contractual Obligation* album)

SI:(1980) Charisma CB 374 (U.K.)

THE GALAXY SONG / EVERY SPERM IS SACRED (1983)
(single from the CBS soundtrack of "Monty Python's The Meaning of Life;" features the same tracks as the over-sized picture disc)

SI:(1983) CBS Records A 3495 (U.K.)

THE GALAXY SONG / EVERY SPERM IS SACRED (1983)
(this is an over-sized picture disc released with tracks from the original CBS recording of "Meaning of Life;" it is shaped like a fishbowl and features a photo of the Python fish from the film)

SI:(1983) CBS Records WA 3495 (U.K.)

ALWAYS LOOK ON THE BRIGHT SIDE OF LIFE / BRIAN SONG (1988)
(reissue of the 1979 single; includes different sleeve, with A-side marked censored and B-side credited to "Sonia Jones")

SI:(1988) Warner Brothers, Warners W 7653 (***)

ALWAYS LOOK ON THE BRIGHT SIDE OF LIFE / I'M SO WORRIED / I BET YOU THEY WON'T PLAY THIS SONG ON THE RADIO (1991)

(LP single, reached No. 3 in U.K. charts)
SI:(1991) Virgin Records Ltd., PYTH 1 (has also been cited as PYTH 1A) (U.K.)

ALWAYS LOOK ON THE BRIGHT SIDE OF LIFE (has also been cited as ALWAYS LOOK ON THE BRIGHT SIDE OF LIFE / I'M SO WORRIED / I BET YOU THEY WON'T PLAY THIS SONG ON THE RADIO / HOLZFALLER SONG) (1991)

(CD Single, reached No. 3 in U.K. charts)
SI:(1991) Virgin Records Ltd., Virgin 9 (has also been cited as PYTH 1) (U.K.)
SI:(1991) Virgin Records Ltd., PYTHD 1 (U.K.) (CD single)
SI:(1991) Virgin Records Ltd., PYTHC 1 (U.K.) (withdrawn yellow cassette single)
SI:(1991) Virgin Records Ltd., PYTHJ 1 (U.K.) (CD single with radio edit of "Always Look on the Bright Side of Life")

ALWAYS LOOK ON THE BRIGHT SIDE OF LIFE / I'M SO WORRIED / I BET YOU THEY WON'T PLAY THIS SONG ON THE RADIO (1991)

(green cassette single, like PYTHC 1 above but without the German "Holzfaller Song")

SI:(1991) Virgin Records Ltd., PYTHR 1 (U.K.)

GALAXY SONG / CHRISTMAS IN HEAVEN / ALWAYS LOOK ON THE BRIGHT SIDE OF LIFE (1991)

(1991 reissue)

SI:(1991) Virgin Records Ltd., PYTH 2 (U.K.)
SI:(1991) Virgin Records Ltd., PYTHD 2 (U.K.) (CD single)
SI:(1991) Virgin Records Ltd., PYTHC 2 (U.K.) (cassette single)

I LIKE CHINESE (1991)
(the catalog number conflicts with single listed above)

SI:(1991) Virgin Records Ltd., PYTHD 2 (U.K.)

I LIKE CHINESE / BRIAN SONG / GALAXY SONG (1992)

SI:(1992) Virgin Records Ltd., 115 260 (Germany) (German 7" single)
SI:(1992) Virgin Records Ltd., 665 260 (Germany) (German CD single)

MONTY PYTHON SPAM SONG / LUMBERJACK SONG (1994)
(included with *The Fairly Incomplete & Rather Badly Illustrated Monty Python Songbook*)

CD: (1994) Virgin Records Ltd. / Kay Gee Bee Music Ltd., Spammy 1 (U.K.)

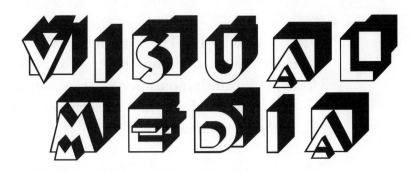

**A.   MONTY PYTHON'S FLYING CIRCUS (THE EPISODES - AMER-
ICAN TAPES)**

**VOL. 1 - THE FIRST MONTY PYTHON'S FLYING CIRCUS VIDEO-
CASSETTE (1970)**

EPISODE 14:   'Face the Press'; New Cooker Sketch / Tobacconists (prostitute advert) / The Ministry of Silly Walks / The Piranha
Brothers.

EPISODE 17:   Architect Sketch / How to Give up Being a Mason /
MotorInsurance Sketch / 'The Bishop' / Living Room on
Pavement / Poets / A Choice of Viewing / Chemist
Sketch / Words Not to be Used Again / After-shave / Vox
Pops / Police Constable Pan-Am.

distributed by Paramount Home Video (1992), PAR 12543 (ISBN 0-7921-0642-3), 60 minutes (includes episodes 14 and 17)

**VOL. 2 - THE SECOND (IN SEQUENCE, NOT QUALITY) MONTY
PYTHON'S FLYING CIRCUS VIDEOCASSETTE (1969 / 1970)**

EPISODE 15:   Man-powered Flight / The Spanish Inquisition / Jokes and Novelties Salesman / Tax on Thingy / Vox Pops / Photos of Uncle Ted (Spanish Inquisition) / The semaphore version of 'Wuthering Heights' / 'Julius Caesar' on an Aldis Lamp / Court Scene (charades).

EPISODE 29:   'The Money Programme' / 'There is Nothing Quite so Wonderful as Money' (song) / Erizabeth L / Fraud Film Squad / Salvation Fuzz / Jungle Restaurant / Apology for violence and nudity / Ken Russell's 'Gardening Club' / The Lost World of Roiurama / Six more minutes of Monty Python's Flying Circus / Argument Clinic / Hitting on the Head Lessons / Inspector Flying Fox of the Yard / One more minute of Monty Python's Flying Circus.

distributed by Paramount Home Video (1992), PAR 12544 (ISBN 0-7921-0644-X), 59 minutes (includes episodes 15 and 29)

VOL. 3 - THE THIRD (BUT STILL DRASTICALLY IMPORTANT ABSOLUTELY NECESSARY TO HAVE) MONTY PYTHON'S FLYING CIRCUS VIDEOCASSETTE (1970 / 1972)

EPISODE 20:   'The Attila the Hun Show' / Attila the Nun / Secretary of State Striptease / Vox Pops on Politicians / Ratcatcher / Wainscotting / Killer sheep / The News for Parrots / The News for Gibbons / Today in Parliament / The News for Wombats / Attila the Bun / The Idiot in Society / Test Match / The Epsom Furniture Race / 'Take Your Pick'.

EPISODE 31:   'Summarize Proust Competition' / Everest Climbed by Hairdressers / Fire Brigade / Our Eamonn / 'Party Hints' with Veronica Smalls / Language Laboratory / Travel

Agent / Watney's Red Barrel / Theory on Brontosauruses by Anne Elk (Miss).

distributed by Paramount Home Video (1986), PAR 12545 (ISBN 0-7921-0646-6), 58 minutes (includes episodes 20 and 31)

VOL. 4 - THE FOURTH (EAGERLY AWAITED, IMPATIENTLY ANTICIPATED, ARDENTLY SOUGHT AFTER, RARING-TO-GO AND REAL GOOD) MONTY PYTHON'S FLYING CIRCUS VIDEOTAPE (1970 / 1972)

EPISODE 22:   'How to Recognize Different Parts of the Body' / Bruces / Naughty Bits / The Man who Contradicts People / Cosmetic Surgery / Camp Square-bashing / Cut-price Airline / Batley Townswomen's Guild Presents the First Heart Transplant / The First Underwater Production of 'Measure for Measure' / The Death of Mary Queen of Scots / Exploding Penguin on the TV Set / There's Been a Murder / Europolice Song Contest / 'Bing Tiddle Tiddle Bong' (song).

EPISODE 28:   Emigration from Surbiton to Hounslow / Schoolboys' Life Assurance Company / How to rid the world of all known diseases / Mrs. Niggerbaiter explodes / Vicar / salesman / Farming Club / 'Life of Tschaikowsky' / Trim-Jeans Theatre / Fish-slapping dance / World War One / The BBC is short of money / Puss in Boots.

distributed by Paramount Home Video (1992), PAR 12560 (ISBN 0-7921-0648-2), 60 minutes (includes episodes 22 and 28)

VOL. 5 - MONTY PYTHON'S FIFTH VIDEOCASSETTE (1970 / 1972)

EPISODE 25:   'The Black Eagle' / Dirty Hungarian Phrasebook / Court (phrasebook) / Communist Quiz / 'Ypres 1914' - Abandoned / Art Gallery Strikes / 'Ypres 1914' / Hospital for Over-actors / Gumby Flower arranging / Spam.

EPISODE 32: Tory Housewives Clean-up Campaign / Gumby Brain Specialist / Mollusks - 'Live' TV Documentary / The Minister for Not Listening to People / Tuesday Documentary / Children's Story / Party Political Broadcast / Apology (politicians) / Expedition to Lake Pahoe / The Silliest Interview We've Ever Had / The Silliest Sketch We've Ever Done.

distributed by Paramount Home Video (1987), PAR 12561 (ISBN 0-7921-0722-5), 59 minutes (includes episodes 25 and 32)

VOL. 6 - VOLUME SIX AND VIOLENCE (1970 / 1972)

EPISODE 24: Conquistador Coffee Campaign / Repeating Groove / Ramsey MacDonald Striptease / Job Hunter / Agatha Christie Sketch (railway timetables) / Mr. Neville Shunte / Film director (teeth) / City Gents Vox Pops / 'Crackpot Religions Ltd.' / 'How not to be seen' / Crossing the Atlantic on a Tricycle / Interview in Filing Cabinet / 'Yummy yummy' / Monty Python's Flying Circus again in thirty seconds.

EPISODE 33: Biggles Dictates a Letter / Climbing the North Face of the Uxbridge Road / Lifeboat / Old lady Snoopers / 'Storage Jars' / The Show so Far / Cheese Shop / Philip Jenkinson on Cheese Westerns / Sam Peckinpah's 'Salad Days' / Apology / The News with Richard Baker / Seashore Interlude Film.

distributed by Paramount Home Video (1987), PAR 12582, 58 minutes (includes episodes 24 and 33)

VOL. 7 - PIPE DREAMS (1970 / 1972)

EPISODE 18: Live from the Grill-o-Mat Snack Bar, Paignton / 'Blackmail' / Society for Putting Things on Top of Other Things / Escape (from film) / Current affairs / Accidents Sketch / Seven Brides for Seven Brothers / The Man who is Alternately Rude and Polite / Documentary on Boxer.

EPISODE 35: Bomb on Plane / A Naked Man / Ten Seconds of Sex / Housing Project Built by Characters from Nineteenth-century English Literature / M1Interchange Built by Characters from 'Paradise Lost' / Mystico and Janet - Flats built by Hypnosis / 'Mortuary Hour' / The Olympic Hide-and-Seek Final / The Cheap-Laughs / Bull-fighting / The British Well-Basically Club / Prices on the Planet Algon.

distributed by Paramount Home Video (1987), PAR 12583, 60 minutes (includes episodes 18 and 35)

VOL. 8 - BEHIND THE EIGHT BALL (1970 / 1972)

EPISODE 26: The Queen Will be Watching / Coal Mine (historical argument) / The Man who says Things in a Very Roundabout Way / The Man who Speaks Only the Ends of Words / The Man who Speaks Only the Beginnings of Words / The Man who Speaks Only the Middles of Words / Commercials / How to Feed a Goldfish / The Man who Collects Birdwatcher's Eggs / Insurance Sketch / Hospital Run by RSM / Mountaineer / Exploding Version of 'The Blue Danube' / Girls Boarding School / Submarine / Lifeboat (cannibalism) / Undertaker's Sketch.

EPISODE 36: Tudor Jobs Agency / Pornographic Bookshop / Elizabethan Pornography Smugglers / Silly Disturbances (the Rev. Arthur Belling) / The Free Repetition of Doubtful Words Sketch, by an Underrated Author / 'Is there?'... Life After Death? / The Man who Says Words in the Wrong Order / Thripshaw's Disease / Silly Noises / Sherry-drinking Vicar.

distributed by Paramount Home Video (1988), PAR 12600 (ISBN 0-7921-0728-4), 58 minutes (includes episodes 26 and 36)

VOL. 9 - SILLY PARTY AND OTHER FAVORS (1970 / 1972)

EPISODE 19: 'It's a Living' / The time on BBC 1 / School Prize-giving / 'if' - A Film by Mr. Dibley / 'Rear Window' - A Film by Mr. Dibley / 'Finian's Rainbow' (starring the Man From the Off-license) / Foreign Secretary / Dung / Dead Indian / Timmy Williams interview / Raymond Luxury Yacht interview / Registry office / Election Night Special (Silly and Sensible Parties).

EPISODE 27: Court Scene (multiple murderer) / Icelandic Saga / Court Scene (Viking) / Stock Exchange Report / Mrs. Premise and Mrs. Conclusion Visit Jean-Paul Sartre / Whicker Island.

distributed by Paramount Home Video (1988), PAR 12601 (ISBN 0-7921-0656-3), 60 minutes (includes episodes 19 and 27)
distributed by Paramount (1991), LV 12601 (ISBN 0-7921-2059-0), 60 minutes (laserdisc number thirteen / includes episodes 19 and 27)

VOL. 10 - BLOOD, DEVASTATION, DEATH, WAR, HORROR, AND OTHER HUMOROUS EVENTS (1970 / 1972)

EPISODE 16: A Bishop Rehearsing / Flying Lessons / Hijacked Plane (to Luton) / The Poet McTeagle / Psychiatrist Milkman / Complaints / Deja vu.

EPISODE 30: 'Blood, Devastation, Death, War and Horror' / The Man who Speaks in Anagrams / Anagram Quiz / Merchant Banker / Pantomime Horses / Life and Death Struggles / Mary Recruitment Office / Bus Conductor Sketch / The Man who Makes People Laugh Uncontrollably / Army Captain as Clown / Gestures to Indicate Pauses in a Televised Talk / Neurotic Announcers / The News with Richard Baker (vision only) / 'The Pantomime Horse is a Secret Agent Film'.

distributed by Paramount Home Video (1988), PAR 12652 (ISBN 0-7921-0602-4), 60 minutes (includes episodes 16 and 30)
distributed by Paramount (19**), LV 12652 (ISBN 0-7291-1568-6), 60 minutes (laserdisc number five / includes episodes 16 and 30)

VOL. 11 - DIRTY VICARS, POOFY JUDGES, AND OSCAR WILDE, TOO! (1970 / 1973)

EPISODE 21: Trailer / 'Archeology Today' / Silly Vicar / Leapy Lee / Registrar (wife swap) / Silly Doctor Sketch (immediately Abandoned) / Mr. and Mrs. Git / Mosquito Hunters / Poofy Judges / Mrs. Thing and Mrs. Entity / Beethoven's Mynah Bird / Shakespeare / Michaelangelo / Colin Mozart (ratcatcher) / Judges.

EPISODE 39: Thames TV Introduction / 'Light Entertainment Awards' / Dickie Attenborough / The Oscar Wilde Sketch / David Niven's Fridge / Pasolini's Film 'The Third Test Match' / New Brain from Curry's / Blood Donor / International Wife-Swapping / Credits of the Year / The dirty Vicar Sketch.

distributed by Paramount Home Video (1992), PAR 12653 (ISBN 0-7921-0604-0), 60 minutes (includes episodes 21 and 39)
distributed by Paramount (19**), LV 12653 (ISBN 0-7291-1569-4), 60 minutes (laserdisc number six / includes episodes 21 and 39)

VOL. 12 - KAMIKAZE HIGHLANDERS (1973)

EPISODE 37:   'Boxing Tonight' - Jack Bodell v. Sir Kenneth Clark / Dennis Moore / Lupins / What the Stars Foretell / Doctor / 'TV4 or Not TV4' discussion / Ideal Loon Exhibition / Off-Licence / 'Prejudice'.

EPISODE 38:   Party Political Broadcast (choreographed) / 'A Book at Bedtime' / 'Redgauntlet' / Kamikaze Scotsmen / No Time to Lose / Penguins / BBC Programme Planners / Unexploded Scotsmen / 'Spot the Looney' / Rival Documentaries / 'Dad's Doctors' (trail) / Dad's Pooves' (trail).

distributed by Paramount Home Video (1988), PAR 12654 (ISBN 0-7921-0606-7), 60 minutes (includes episodes 37 and 38)
distributed by Paramount (19**), LV 12654 (ISBN 0-7291-1570-8), 60 minutes (laserdisc number seven; includes episodes 37 and 38)

VOL. 13 - I'M A LUMBERJACK, (1969)

EPISODE 1:   'It's Wolfgang Amadeus Mozart' / Famous Deaths / Italian Lesson / Whizzo Butter / 'It's the Arts' / Arthur 'Two-Sheds' Jackson / Picasso / Cycling Race / The Funniest Joke in the World.

EPISODE 9:   Llamas / A Man with a Tape Recorder up his Nose / Kilimanjaro Expedition (double vision) / A Man with a Tape Recorder up his Brother's Nose / Homicidal Barber / Lumberjack Song / Gumby Crooner / The Refreshment Room at Bletchley / Hunting Film / The Visitors.

distributed by Paramount Home Video (1989), PAR 12736 (ISBN 0-7921-2363-8), 60 minutes (includes episodes 1 and 9)
distributed by Paramount (19**), LV 12736 (ISBN 0-7291-1571-6), 60 minutes (laserdisc number eight; includes episodes 1 and 9)

VOL. 14 - CHOCOLATE FROGS, BAFFLED CATS, AND OTHER TASTY TREATS (1969)

EPISODE 5: Confuse-a-Cat / The Smuggler / A Duck, a Cat and a Lizard (discussion) / Vox Pops on Smuggling / Police Raid / Letters and Vox Pops / Newsreader Arrested / Erotic Film / Silly Job Interview / Careers Advisory Board / Burglar / Encyclopedia Salesman.

EPISODE 6: 'It's the Arts' / Johann Gombolputty... von Hautkopf of Ulm / Non-illegal Robbery / Vox Pops / Crunchy Frog / The Dull Life of a City Stockbroker / Red Indian in Theatre / Policemen Make Wonderful Friends / A Scotsman on a Horse / Twentieth-century Vole.

distributed by Paramount Home Video (1989), PAR 12737 (ISBN 0-7921-1008-0), 60 minutes (includes episodes 5 and 6)
distributed by Paramount (19**), LV 12736 (ISBN 0-7291-1572-4), 60 minutes (laserdisc number nine; includes episodes 5 and 6)

VOL. 15 - DEAD PARROTS DON'T TALK AND OTHER FOWL PLAYS (1969)

EPISODE 7: Camel Spotting / You're no Fun Any More / The Audit / Science Fiction Sketch / Man Turns into Scotsman / Police Station / Blancmanges Playing Tennis.

EPISODE 8: Army Protection Racket / Vox Pops / Art Critic - the Place of the Nude / Buying a Bed / Hermits / Dead Parrot / The Flasher / Hell's Grannies.

distributed by Paramount Home Video (1989), PAR 12738 (ISBN 0-7921-1010-2), 60 minutes (includes episodes 7 and 8)

distributed by Paramount (19**), LV 12738 (ISBN **********), 60 minutes (laserdisc number ten; includes episodes 7 and 8)

VOL. 16 - A MAN WITH THREE CHEEKS, OR BUTT NAUGHT FOR ME (1969)

EPISODE 2:   Flying Sheep / French Lecture on Sheep-aircraft / A Man with Three Buttocks / A Man with Two Noses / Musical Mice / Marriage Guidance Counselor / The Wacky Queen / Working-class Playwright / A Scotsman on a Horse / The Wrestling Epilogue / The Mouse Problem.

EPISODE 11:   Letter (lavatorial humour) / Interruptions / Agatha Christie Sketch / Literary Football Discussion / Undertakers Film / Interesting People / Eighteenth-century Social Legislation / The Battle of Trafalgar / Batley Townswomens' Guild Presents the Battle of Pearl Harbor / Undertakers film.

distributed by Paramount Home Video (1989), PAR 12739 (ISBN 0-7921-1012-9), 60 minutes (includes episodes 2 and 11)

distributed by Paramount (19**), LV 12739 (ISBN 0-7921-1575-9), 60 minutes (laserdisc number eleven ; includes episodes 2 and 11)

VOL. 17 - THE UPPER-CLASS TWIT COMPETITION (1970)

EPISODE 12:   Falling from Building / 'Spectrum' - Talking About Things / Visitors from Coventry / Mr. Hilter / The Minehead By-election / Police Station (silly voices) / Upperclass Twit of the Year / Ken Shabby / How far can a Minister Fall?

EPISODE 13:   Intermissions / Restaurant (abuse / cannibalism) / Advertisements / Albatross / Come Back to My Place /

Me Doctor / Historical Impersonations / Quiz Programme - 'Wishes' / 'Probe-around' On Crime / Stonehenge / Mr. Attila the Hun / Psychiatry - Silly Sketch / Operating Theatre (squatters).

distributed by Paramount Home Video (1989), PAR 12740 (ISBN 0-7921-1014-5), 60 minutes (includes episodes 12 and 13)
distributed by Paramount (1990), LV 12740 (ISBN 0-7921-1575-9), 60 minutes (laserdisc number twelve; includes episodes 12 and 13)

VOL. 18 - DESPICABLE FAMILIES, NAUGHTY COMPLAINTS, AND KILLER FRUIT (1969 / 1974)

EPISODE 4:   Song ('And did those feet') / Art Gallery / Art Critic / It's a Man's Life in the Modern Army / Undressing in Public / Self-defense / Secret Service Dentists.

EPISODE 45:   'Most Awful Family in Britain' / Icelandic Honey Week / A Doctor Whose Patients are Stabbed by his Nurse / Brigadier and Bishop / Appeal on Behalf of Extremely Rich People / The Man who Finishes Other People's Sentences / David Attenborough / The Walking Tree of Dahomey / The Batsmen of the Kalahari / Cricket Match (assegais) / BBC News (handovers).

distributed by Paramount Home Video (1990), PAR 12765 (ISBN 0-7921-1908-8), 60 minutes (includes episodes 4 and 45)

VOL. 19 - NUDGE, NUDGE, WINK, WINK (1969 / 1974)

EPISODE 3:   Court Scene (Witness in Coffin / Cardinal Richelieu) / The Larch / Bicycle Repair Man / Children's Stories / Restaurant Sketch / Seduced Milkmen / Stolen Newsreader / Children's Interview / Nudge Nudge.

EPISODE 43: Bogus Psychiatrists / 'Nationwide' / Police Helmets / Father-in-Law / Hamlet and Ophelia / Boxing Match Aftermath / Boxing Commentary / Piston Engine (a bargain) / A Room in Polonius' House / Dentists / Live from Epsom / Queen Victoria Handicap.

distributed by Paramount Home Video (1990), PAR 12766 (ISBN 0-7921-1910-X), 60 minutes (includes episodes 3 and 19)

VOL. 20 - PET ANTS, DEAD POETS & THE MYSTERIOUS MICHAEL ELLIS (1969 / 1974)

EPISODE 10: Walk-on part in sketch / Bank Robber (lingerie shop) / Trailer / Arthur Tree / Vocational Guidance Counselor (chartered accountant) / The First Man to Jump the Channel / Tunneling from Godalming to Java / Pet Conversions / Gorilla Librarian / Letters to 'Daily Mirror' / Strangers in the Night.

EPISODE 41: Department Store / Buying an Ant / At Home with the Ant and Other Pets / Documentary on Ants / Ant Communication / Poetry Reading (ants) / Toupee / Different Endings.

distributed by Paramount Home Video (1990), PAR 12767 (ISBN 0-7921-1912-6), 60 minutes (includes episodes 10 and 41)

VOL. 21 - SCOTT OF THE ANTARCTIC (1970 / 1974)

EPISODE 23: French subtitled film / Scott of the Antarctic / Scott of the Sahara / Fish License / Derby Council v. All Blacks Rugby Match / Long John Silver Impersonators v. Bournemouth Gynecologists.

EPISODE 42:   'Up your Pavement' / RAF Banter / Trivializing the War / Courtmartial / Basingstoke in Westphalia / 'Anything Goes In' (song) / Film trailer / The Public are Idiots / Programme Titles Conference / The Last Five Miles of the M2 / Woody and Tinny Words / Show-jumping (musical) / Newsflash (Germans) / 'When Does A Dream Begin?' (song).

distributed by Paramount Home Video (1990), PAR 12768 (ISBN 0-7921-1914-2), 60 minutes (includes episodes 23 and 42)

VOL. 22 - MR. NEUTRON'S BALLOONISH BICYCLE TOUR (1972 / 1974)

EPISODE 40:   Montgolfier Brothers / Louis XIV / George III / Zeppelin.

EPISODE 44:   Post box ceremony / Teddy Salad (CIA agent) / 'Conjuring Today'.

distributed by Paramount Home Video (1990), PAR 12770 (ISBN 0-7921-1916-9), 90 minutes (includes episodes 34, 40, and 44)

MONTY PYTHON'S FLIEGENDER ZIRKUS (1971 / 1972)
(contains both German Fliegender Zirkus episodes "Monty Python in Deutschland" (1971) and "Monty Python Blodeln fur Deutschland" (1972); filmed for Germany's Bavaria Atlier television of Munich / the first episode is entirely in German, which the Pythons had to learn phonetically, with English subtitles, while the second episode is in its original English; this particular tape has been available through Australian distributors and is only playable in PAL mode).

SHOW EINS: An Introduction to Monty Python By Frau Newsreader / The Journey of The Olympic Flame / Monty Python's

Guide to Albrecht Durer / Anita Ekberg Sings Albrecht Durer / The Merchant of Venice / Little Red Riding Hood / The History of Comedy / Stake Your Claim / The Lumberjack Song with The Austrian Border Police

SHOW ZWIE: William Tell / Euro Sex Maniacs / The Sycophancy Show / Mouse Reserve / Fish Park / Chicken Mining / Football Match – Greeks v Germans / Wrestling Match - Colin "Bomber" Harris v Colin "Bomber" Harris / 10 Seconds of Sex / I Want A Hearing Aid / The Tale of Happy Valley (The Princess with The Wooden Teeth)

BMG Video, 74321 36100 3, 86 minutes (includes both German episodes)

MONTY PYTHON AT THE MOVIES
AND NOW FOR SOMETHING COMPLETELY DIFFERENT (1971)
(Monty Python's first film; a collection of their most popular sketches and animations which were re-filmed for five weeks in October and November 1970 at a former dairy in north London)

Columbia Pictures / Kettledrum-Python Productions Film, distributed by RCA / Columbia Pictures Home Video (1991), 43396 6013 (ISBN 0-8001-1171-0), 88 minutes
Columbia Pictures / Kettledrum-Python Productions Film, (U.K.) CC7149, 88 minutes

AND NOW FOR SOMETHING COMPLETELY DIFFERENT (1971)
(laser disc version of the film; presented in the original (letterbox) theatrical aspect ratio of 1.66 to 1; a review from Time Magazine (May 26, 1975) is printed on the back cover; the sketches are chaptered into 35 segments; the disc is in extended play (CLV) format which also allows chapter search)

Columbia Pictures / Kettledrum-Python Productions Film, distributed by Columbia Tristar Home Video (1994), 76826 (ISBN 0-8001-3813-9), 89 minutes

MONTY PYTHON AND THE HOLY GRAIL (1974)
(Monty Python's first successful full-length feature film; traces King Arthur's

quest for the Holy Grail with his Knights of Round Table; filmed in Scotland, it is a true classic and perennial favorite on college campuses)

Cineplex Corp., distributed by Pan-Canadian Video (1983, 1984), **, 92 minutes
Almi-Cinema 5 / Python Pictures-Michael White Film, distributed by RCA / Columbia Pictures Home Video (1991), 43396 92253 (ISBN 0-8001-1329-2), 90 minutes
Almi-Cinema 5 / Python Pictures-Michael White Film, distributed by Brent Walker Video (19***), ***, 90 minutes
RCA Videodisc, RCA / 03040 / 1974, 96 minutes

MONTY PYTHON AND THE HOLY GRAIL (1974)
(special laser disc version of the film; includes a "coming attraction" trailer, a bonus 24-second sequence from "The Tale of Sir Galahad" not previously released, an analog track featuring audio commentary by Terry Gilliam and Terry Jones, another analog track featuring the entire movie dubbed in Japanese, and various silly photos taken on location during the film's production; shown in its original aspect ratio of 1.85 to 1)

National Film Trustee Company, Ltd., distributed by The Voyager Company and Columbia / Tristar Home Video (1992), *The Criterion Collection*, CC 1311L (ISBN 1-55940-324-1), 91 minutes

MONTY PYTHON AND THE HOLY GRAIL: 21ST ANNIVERSARY EDITION (1974)
(the 21st anniversary edition of *Monty Python and the Holy Grail*, digitally remastered and featuring the missing 24-second Castle Anthrax scene as well as the theatrical trailer; it is only playable in PAL mode)

National Film Trustee Company Ltd., distributed by 20th Century Fox Home Entertainment (1996), 2146C, 89 minutes

MONTY PYTHON AND THE HOLY GRAIL: WIDESCREEN EDITION (1974)
(American widescreen edition of the film; presented in the original theatrical aspect ratio of 1.75:1)
National Film Trustee Company Ltd., distributed by Columbia Tristar Home Video (1997) 22623 (ISBN 0-8001-3799-X), 92 minutes

MONTY PYTHON'S LIFE OF BRIAN (1979)

(Monty Python's second major movie success; filmed entirely on location in Tunisia from September 16 to November 12, 1978; film is about a man in biblical times who is mistaken for a messiah; funding problems for the film led to the creation of Handmade Films by George Harrison and Dennis O'Brien which later produced a number of other Python-related films: *Monty Python Live at the Hollywood Bowl, Time Bandits, Privates on Parade, Nuns on the Run, A Private Function,* and *The Missionary*).

Warner Brothers / Orion Pictures, Handmade Films, distributed by Paramount Home Video (1990), PAR 12871 (ISBN 0-7921-1904-5), 94 minutes
Warner Brothers / Orion Pictures, Handmade Films, distributed by Warner Home Video (19***), 2003, 94 minutes

MONTY PYTHON'S LIFE OF BRIAN (1979)

(the Criterion Collection version of Life of Brian, available only on laserdisc; includes a new digital widescreen transfer approved by Terry Jones; two commentary tracks featuring John Cleese, Terry Gilliam, Eric Idle Terry Jones, and Michael Palin; original theatrical trailer; original radio advertisements; deleted scenes with audio commentary; documentary film *The Pythons* shot on location during the making of *Life of Brian*)

Anchor Bay Entertainment, distributed by The Voyager Company (1997), *"The Criterion Collection",* CC 1504L (ISBN 1-55940-849-9), 94 minutes

MONTY PYTHON LIVE AT THE HOLLYWOOD BOWL (1982)

(film of the stage show performed at the Hollywood Bowl during September 26-29, 1980; their most elaborate presentation of their stage show ever; also contains material from *Monty Python's Contractual Obligation* album which was released earlier that year)

Handmade Films and Columbia Pictures, distributed by Paramount Home Video (1991), PAR 12872 (ISBN 0-7921-1906-1), 81 minutes

MONTY PYTHON'S THE MEANING OF LIFE (1983)

(Monty Python's biggest budget production ever; filmed during the summer of 1982 at a variety of locations in England and Scotland as well as the EMI-Elstree studios in Borehamwood, England; the film is actually a series of sketches linked by a common theme; includes a short film by Terry Gilliam: "The Crimson Permanent Assurance".)

Celandine Films, distributed by MCA Universal Home Video (1991), 71016 (ISBN 1-55880-676-8), 107 minutes
Celandine Films, distributed by MCA Universal Home Video (1996), 71016 (ISBN 1-55880-676-8), 108 minutes

FILMS ABOUT MONTY PYTHON

MONTY PYTHON MEETS BEYOND THE FRINGE (has also been cited as BEYOND THE FRINGE) (1976)

(unauthorized film that consisted of a Dudley Moore-narrated television documentary on the 1976 Amnesty International benefit (*Pleasure at Her Majesty's*) with the backstage scenes edited out)

distributed by Video Communications, Inc., **, 85 minutes
distributed by Wizard Video / F.H.E. Inc. (1982), No. 0040, 85 minutes

LIFE OF PYTHON (1990)

(one hour documentary on Monty Python on the occasion of their 20th anniversary; includes clips from the shows and the films as well as interviews with John Cleese, Terry Gilliam, Eric Idle, Terry Jones, Michael Palin, Steve Martin, Dan Aykroyd, Chevy Chase, and Barry Took; reveals much about the history of the group as well as the origins of some of the more popular sketches)

distributed by Paramount Home Video, PAR 12903 (ISBN 0-7921-2556-8), 56 minutes

MONTY PYTHON'S PARROT SKETCH NOT INCLUDED (1990)

(a collection of some of the best sketches from the Monty Python television series as well as some sketches from the German television episodes; hosted by Steve Martin; all six Pythons make an appearance during the last minute when Steve Martin opens a closet to reveal the troupe hiding there)
distributed by Paramount Home Video, PAR 12904 (ISBN 0-7921-2562-2), 75 minutes

(U.K.), 2940, 75 minutes

COMPUTER SOFTWARE

MONTY PYTHON'S FLYING CIRCUS: THE COMPUTER GAME (1991)

(a computer game where you control D.P. Gumby and his search for four pieces of his missing brain. Pilot him in various incarnations through a labyrinth of Pythonesque obstacles, such as: cheese, vikings, dead parrots, keep left signs, the Spanish Inquisition, half-bees named Eric, soft cushions, and much more; along the way, Mr. Gumby must collect Spam, sausages, eggs, Spam, baked beans, and Spam; if he collects enough he will earn a piece of his brain back; read about this game in the *Daily Llama* Vol. 1 No 4)

Virgin Mastertronic, (ISBN 52145-20154) (IBM / ATARI ST / AMIGA / COMMODORE 64 & 128)

MONTY PYTHON'S COMPLETE WASTE OF TIME (1994)

(interactive CD-ROM for the PC and Macintosh set up as a series of games; features new material provided by Terry Gilliam, Eric Idle, Terry Jones, and Michael Palin; navigate through the lobes of Mrs. Zambesi's brain and interact with images and characters from countless *Flying Circus* sketches; read about this title in the Daily Llama Vol. 1 No 3; also visit 7th Level's Official Complete Waste of Time website)

7th Level, Inc., 70033 (ISBN 0-9641098-3-2) (PC)
7th Level, Inc., 70146 (ISBN 0-887889-00-0) (Macintosh version does not include the Python phone messages) (Macintosh)

MONTY PYTHON'S FLYING CIRCUS DESKTOP PYTHONIZER (1994)

(program which allows you to add Monty Python sounds, pictures, interactive screen savers, etc. to your Windows environment; does not include as many Pythonizer items as the CD-ROM however.)

7th Level, Inc., 70038 (ISBN 0-9641098-4-0) (six floppy diskette version; does not include as many Pythonizer items as the CD-ROM) (PC)
7th Level, Inc., 70064 (CD-ROM version which contains the same material as the Pythonizer on the Complete Waste of Time CD) (PC)

MONTY PYTHON'S FLYING CIRCUS DESKTOP PYTHONIZER: MONTY PYTHON'S LIMITED EDITION DESKTOP EXTRAS (1994)

(single floppy disk with additional Pythonizer modules; comes free upon submitting the registration card for the "Complete Waste of Time" CD-ROM and / or the "Desktop Pythonizer")

7th Level, Inc., 70041

VIDEO ARTS CD-i PROGRAMS (1991)

(interactive compact discs for the Philips CD-i player available from Video Arts, featuring sequences with John Cleese from his training videos. Additional CD-i titles are available; to order, call 1-800-553-0091 or 1-312-693-0500; or visit the Video Arts Home Page)

Meetings, Blood Meetings - John Cleese plays a manager who is put on trial for negligent conduct of meetings, before a courtroom run according to his haphazard regard to rules.
It's Your Choice - John Cleese as "Ivan the Terrible," a manager with poor interviewing skills who causes the wrong person to be hired.
Straight Talking - John Cleese shows the techniques of assertive behavior in a series of settings and how it does not always guarantee success.
How to Lose Customers Without Really Trying - a series of sketches, featur-

ing John Cleese, showing how customer care is crucial to an organization's reputation.

More Bloody Meetings - a sequel to the last "meetings" film, John Cleese again plays the manager who, during a trip to the dentists, dreams that the office has become an interrogation room.

The Helping Hand - Coaching Skills for Managers - John Cleese plays the presenter in a training video on coaching; unfortunately his fictional video features a manager who knows absolutely nothing about coaching.

The Unorganized Manager - a manager is confronted by St. Peter, played by John Cleese, who sends him back to Earth with a list of his eleven deadly organizational sins.

Telephone Behavior - The Power and the Perils - video presented by John Cleese on how people's behavior can either wreck a telephone conversation or make it into a highly effective piece of communication.

CRITERION GOES TO THE MOVIES (1993)

(an interactive guide to Voyager Company's Criterion laser disc collection; includes entries on most of the films, including liner notes, essays, pictures, film synopses, and film clips; includes clips from *The Adventures of Baron Munchausen* and *The Fisher King*).

The Voyager Company (1993), CDRM 1112350 (ISBN 1559402636) (Macintosh)
The Voyager Company (1993), CDRM (PC / Windows)

LIVE (LIFE) WITH(OUT) MONTY PYTHON (1994)

(interactive compact disc for the Philips / Magnavox CD-i player; features karaoke songs and sketches where you can sing or participate in popular sketches like the Dead Parrot sketch and the Argument Clinic; released November of 1994 in Europe; read about it in the Daily Llama Vol. 1 No 7)

TRACK LISTING:
Always Look on the Bright Side of Life / Lumberjack Song / Every Sperm is Sacred / I've Got Two Legs / The Meaning of Life / Money Song / Bruce's

Philosopher's Song / Accountancy Shanty / Camelot Song / Penis Song / Dennis Moore Theme / Sit On My Face / Galaxy Song / Never Be Rude to an Arab / Brian Song / Argument Clinic / Parrot Sketch
Daedalus CD-i Productions (Amsterdam) (1994), 819 1008 (CD-i)
MORE NAUGHTY BITS (1994)
(interactive compact disc for the Philips; Magnavox CD-i player / some of the best sketches with optional subtitles in four different languages. Includes the Bavarian restaurant sketch from the German television series; released November of 1994 in Europe; read about it in *Daily Llama* Vol. 1 No 7)

TRACK LISTING:
Black Knight / Trojan Rabbit / What Have the Romans Ever Done For Us / Fat Man (Mr. Creosote) / Four Yorkshireman / BRian / Nudge Nudge / Dirty Fork / Silly Job Interview / Dead Parrot / Kilimanjaro / Ministry of Silly Walks / Spanish Inquisition / Dirty Hungarian Phrasebook / Argument Clinic / Merchant Banker / Das Bayerisches Restaurant Stück

Daedalus CD-i Productions (Amsterdam) (1994), 819 1006 (CD-i)

THE INVASION OF THE PLANET SKYRON (1995)
(title for the Philips CD-i player in which you play Pythonesque arcade games in nine different Terry Gilliam-cartoon environments; the game also features full-motion video clips from the *Monty Python* television series which serve as rewards for completing the games; read about this title in *Daily Llama* Vol. 1 No 7)

Daedalus CD-i Productions (Amsterdam) (1995), 819 1007 (CD-i)

MONTY PYTHON'S COMPLETE WASTE OF TIME: AN OFFICIAL COMPENDIUM OF ANSWERS TO RUDDY QUESTIONS NOT NORMALLY CONSIDERED RELEVANT TO MOUNTIES! by Rusel Demaria and Alex Uttermann
(a terrific hintbook for *"Monty Python's Complete Waste of Time"* CD-ROM game. Comes complete with maps, illustrations, and instructions on what to

do in each of the lobes of the brain as you search for the secret to intergalactic success. Profusely illustrated with Python graphics and other fun stuff. Hints can also obtained at 7th Level, Inc.'s web site.)

Prima Publishing, 1995 (U.S.) ISBN 0-7615-0139-8 (paperback)

MONTY PYTHON AND THE HOLY GRAIL (19***)
(text adventure-based game for the Commodore 64 and ZX Spectrum 48k; very little information is available on this title except that it is known to exist; if you have any information, please e-mail me at htencate@erols.com)

No additional information is currently available

DISCWORLD (1995)
(animated interactive CD-ROM game based on Terry Pratchett's Discworld books; player controls the character Rincewind in his attempts to save the city of Ankh-Morpork from a dragon; Eric Idle performs the voice of Rincewind)

Psygnosis / Perfect 10 Productions (1995), (ISBN 53203-01328) (PC)
Psygnosis / Perfect 10 Productions (1995), (Macintosh version is not compatible with all Mac models) (Macintosh)
Psygnosis / Perfect 10 Productions (1995), (Sony Playstation)

TERRY PRATCHETT'S DISCWORLD: THE OFFICIAL STRATEGY GUIDE, Glen Edridge
(complete strategy guide which includes all of the official secrets to completing the game; includes a full-color map of Ankh-Morpork and scenes from the game)

Prima Publishing, 1995 (U.S.) ISBN 0-7615-0218-1 (paperback)
Prima Publishing, 1995 (U.K.) ISBN 0-55214-439-8 (***)

JOURNEYMAN PROJECT 2: BURIED IN TIME (1995)
(a graphic-adventure game which has several Monty Python references; one involves a medieval castle in France where the main character's digital assistant yells: "I fart in your general direction. Your mother was a 'amster and your father smelt

of elderberries!" In another scene, if the agent hesitates too long in front of the castle guards, he is crushed by a live cow: "He found himself an unwilling participant in the re-enactment of a silly Monty Python skit!")

Sanctuary Woods / Presto Studios (1995), (ISBN 1-55182-036-6) (Macintosh)
MONTY PYTHON'S QUEST FOR THE HOLY GRAIL (1996)
(the second Monty Python CD-ROM game to come out of 7th Level; produced by Eric Idle with new contributions by the members of Monty Python; guide King Arthur and his silly knights across the English countryside in search of the Holy Grail; play silly games and find hidden clues; plays just like the movie!; limited edition features unique packaging with the signatures of the six Pythons on the front and on the disc; read about this game in *Daily Llama Issues* Vol. 1 / No 3 and Vol. 1 / No 11; Visit 7th

Level's Holy Grail Web Site for even more information
7th Level, Inc., 70241 (ISBN 1-887889-17-5) (PC)
7th Level, Inc., 70320 (ISBN 1-887889-21-3) (Macintosh)

BLAZING DRAGONS (1996)
(Terry Jones' hilarious medieval adventure game for the Sony Playstation; you play the role of Flicker, a dragon who must save Camelot from the evil knight, Sir George; lots of funny Pythonesque sequences and subplots; features the voices of Terry Jones, Harry Shearer, and Cheech Marin; read about it in *Daily Llama* Vol. 1 No. 4 or visit the Crystal Dynamics homepage)

Crystal Dynamics, distributed by Mindscape (1996), SLUS-00100 (ISBN 0-7911-2578-5) (Sony Playstation)

DISCWORLD II: MISSING PRESUMED...!? (1997)
(sequel to the successful and very funny adventure game "Discworld"; Eric Idle reprises the role of Rincewind, a wizard, who must help find the Grim Reaper because Death has apparently forgotten his chief duty: to collect human souls; includes an original song, "That's Death", written and performed by Eric Idle; other voice-overs were provided by Nigel Planer, Kate Robins and Rob Brydon; visit the Psygnosis web page for more info)

Psygnosis / Perfect 10 Productions (1997), (UK version is titled "Discworld II: Missing Presumed...!?") (PC)
Psygnosis / Perfect 10 Productions (1997), (US version is titled "Discworld II: Mortality Bytes!") (PC)

MONTY PYTHON'S THE MEANING OF LIFE (1997)
(the third Monty Python CD-ROM game, with new material provided by Terry Gilliam, Eric Idle, Terry Jones, Michael Palin, and John Cleese; you search for the meaning of life in an ever-increasingly-more-difficult series of clue searches and games; features lots of never-before-seen Python animations, full-motion clips from the movie, and an interactive tour of Terry Gilliam's studio in his London home; this is the first Monty Python title to be sold by the new distributor, Panasonic Interactive Media)

Panasonic Interactive Media (1997), PIM-10028 (PC)

DOUGLAS ADAMS STARSHIP TITANIC (1998)
(an interactive adventure game developed by renowned author and humorist Douglas Adams; combines stunning graphics with an artificially intelligent text parser for an unpredictable ride aboard the Starship Titanic, the ship that just couldn't go wrong; interact with a variety of odd characters including a parrot, voiced by Terry Jones; Jones also collaborated with Adams to write the novel based on the game)

The Digital Village, Ltd. / Simon & Schuster Interactive (1998), (ISBN 0-671-55025-X) (PC)

DOUGLAS ADAMS STARSHIP TITANIC: THE OFFICIAL STRATEGY GUIDE, by Neil Richards
(very well illustrated guide to the *Starship Titanic* game, which features the voice of Terry Jones; lots of illustrations, photos, and maps; organized so that you don't receive the solutions to puzzles that haven't started to puzzle you yet; includes an introduction by Douglas Adams and an interview with Adams that explains how Terry Jones became involved in the project)

Three Rivers Press, 1998 (U.S.) ISBN 0-609-80147-3 (paperback)
Pan Books, 1998 (U.K.) ISBN 0-330-35447-7 (paperback)

MONTY PYTHON'S LOONEY BIN (1998)
(a software bundle of *Monty Python's Complete Waste of Time, Monty Python & The Quest for the Holy Grail,* and *Desktop Pythonizer* in new packaging; presented by Panasonic Interactive Media, who took over the distribution rights for the Monty Python products)

Panasonic Interactive Media (1998), PIM-10035 (PC)

QUEST FOR CAMELOT: DRAGON GAMES (1998)
(seven interactive games for kids, ages 5 to 10; based on the *Quest for Camelot* animated film by Warner Brothers, which starred Eric Idle as the voice of Devon; although the characters Devon and Cornwall are voiced by two other actors in this CD ROM game, there are plenty of film clips which feature the original Eric Idle / Don Rickles voices)

Funnybone Interactive / Knowledge Adventure (1998), (ISBN 1-56997-338-5)

CARDS (COLLECTIBLE, GREETING)
MONTY PYTHON'S FLYING CIRCUS TRADING CARDS - ACT 1
(Cornerstone Communication's first set of trading cards featuring photographs, artwork, and video stills from the original television series; created for the 25th anniversary of Monty Python in October 1994; 114 cards total in this set; read about the cards in *Daily Llama* Vol. 1 No. 11; for more information or to order, call 1-800-846-7725 or visit Cornerstone Communication's home page)
Cornerstone Communications, 1994

MONTY PYTHON AND THE HOLY GRAIL - VERY WIDE TRADING CARDS
(Cornerstone Communication's second series of trading cards; released in 1996, this series is entirely based on the film *Monty Python and the Holy Grail* and was produced from an original print of the film; 76 cards total in this set; read the complete story of the Holy Grail trading card series in the *Daily Llama*

Vol. 1 No 11; for more information or to order, call 1-800-846-7725 or visit Cornerstone Communication's home page)

Cornerstone Communications, 1996

MONTY PYTHON AND THE HOLY GRAIL - THE COLLECTIBLE CARD GAME

(Kenzer & Co. created this collectible card game, or CCG, in 1995; there are 314 different cards available which you can collect as trading cards and then use in games against opponents; lots of silly rules and cards with Pythonesque abilities; read about the card game in *Daily Llama* Vol. 1 No 12; also, visit the Official Monty Python and the Holy Grail CCG website maintained by Kenzer & Company)

Kenzer & Company, 1995

On the set of
'Brian'. Graham poses
with a body double
for the spaceship
sequence.

DO NOT ADJUST YOUR SET: A HYGIENIC VIEW

by 'Legs' Larry Smith

Somewhat surprisingly, the day of the studio shoot would invariably begin at Paddington Station, a large railway station in London. I would wake (with hangover) tucked up inside a stuffy overnight "sleeper" compartment whose temperature was hot enough to boil an egg.

A pot of hateful early morning tea would be pushed under my large nose; tea strong enough to preserve Piltdown Man for another 1,000 years or more, and I would peer out of a steamed up window at a world-full of marching peepel who'd already managed to grab a 10 yard start on me.

Bonzo Dog were working hard, (see above) entertaining the troops, blowing kisses, boozing, barking, banging their heads together and blowing things up (on-stage of course)—traveling all over the wretched place. We seemed to be permanently onboard some kind of "modular vehicle of transported delight." The point being, there were simply too many gigs being thrust upon us (by our adoring management) and it was getting harder for the band to remain *Alpine-fresh* in its approach (and deserved commitment) to dear old "Do Not Adjust Your Trousers" (as we called it). We were always turning up at the studios completely "shagged-out" (as they say), and it was becoming ever more difficult to be constantly and ferociously fabulous (without the aid of a good strong *laxative, that is).

The tension and the hateful stresses (see above) associated with the (frankly) demanding world of Television were already there, you see. Building, building, growing and growing. Growing like the blue-grey mold on an old Boston Hershey Bar. Not between cast members (naturally, we were all terribly in love with each other and took every Cod-given opportunafish to tell each other so), but the real trouble, the real problem, began with Irene Cuttlefish and her lurid daughter, Tina.

Tina had begun accompanying her mother to the highly glamorous Television studios in order to seduce (in my opinion) as many attractive young men, stars, musicians, studio technicians, producers, cameramen, photographers, artists, builders, barbers, deep-sea divers, pilots, zoo-keepers, gas-fire repair men, farmers, welding engineers, farm labourers, jockeys, mountaineers and local members of parliament as possible. You see, Tina - Tina was a

**prostitute!! There - I've said it. Names (professions) have been changed, withheld, stolen, forgotten, or even deep-fried in a light crumb-crisp coating in order to preserve the innocent and the decent amongst you, but I felt that this 'quirky' little story simply had to be told.

And Tina - what of Tina? I dream of Tina with the light brown teeth and those metal guards (eight layers!) that her stupid mother made her wear. She would've had such an attractive smile without them. It's a funny old world. You can present pee-pel with a glass of water, but you can't make them drink it.

'Legs' Larry Smith
October 1998

* (NOTE: Taking strong laxatives or any form of muscle relaxant, especially when preparing to shoot "live Television" was rightly (and deservedly) frowned upon by the executive board of Thames Television.)

(**More on Tina, later. Ed.)

PRE-PYTHON: WHEN BONZOS WALKED THE EARTH

No history of *Monty Python's Flying Circus* would be complete (and I would certainly be remiss) without mentioning the comic godparents of the series, the fabulously mad musical / comedy group, The Bonzo Dog (Doo-Dah) Band. Inextricably tied to Python, both in style and in content, the Bonzos helped lead the way towards mass acceptance of prime 60s British silliness. In tunes like 'The Canyons Of Your Mind', 'The Intro and the Outro' and 'My Pink Half of the Drainpipe', the Bonzos deluged the public with their odd preoccupations (shirts, trousers, concrete coal bunkers, and parrots), and prepared the world for future Python obsessions such as sheep, penguins, bishops, and (yes) parrots.

The Bonzo Dog Band was the brain-child of artist / sculptor Vivian Stanshall and Rodney Slater, and they first appeared on the London scene in 1966 as a ricky-tick fox-trot band playing pubs like The Bird In Hand and The Tiger's Head. Vivian Stanshall: 'It all started off more or less by accident. We were all at art school in London, playing together from time to time, when one Easter holiday we were spotted by the chap who booked bands for most of the Northern (England) clubs. He smoked a big fat cigar and asked us if we wanted to be stars.'

Typical of the Bonzos, during the era of 'raga-rock' and the feverish earnestness of the budding young psychedelic sound, they were busy playing traditional jazz tunes like 'Tiger Rag' and 'Bill Bailey Won't You Please Come Home'. But there was nothing traditional about the way that they played them. On stage the band was raucous and funny, often interweaving elaborate stunts, gags and sketches into the music and (at the appropriate time) they would take solos on odd instruments like the spoons, the tuba or the 'electric shirt collar.' (The latter was an invention of Roger Ruskin-Spear, the inventor of robots and phantom saxophonist of the band.)

Many Bonzos came and went during their brief four year span of existence, but the nucleus of the band consisted of Vivian Stanshall (vocals, trumpet); Neil Innes (vocals, piano, guitar); 'Legs' Larry Smith (drums, tap-dancing, vocals); Rodney Slater (saxophones, guitar, vocals); Dennis Cowan (bass and vocals); and Roger Ruskin-Spear (saxophones, guitar, piano and vocals). Roger Ruskin-Spear: 'We started by specializing in 20s music because we all took an interest in it. In those days the outfit was sometimes 30 strong and included as many as 10 banjos and a couple of trumpets all at one time. We lost a lot of members along the way.'

One such 'lost' Bonzo is bassist Joel Druckman, the only American ever to be a member of this most definitive of British bands. Joel Druckman: 'I didn't know who these guys were. I showed up in England with aspirations of playing with Clapton or John Mayall. I saw this article in *Melody Maker*: "BONZO DOG EATS BASS PLAYER!" so I somehow get a hold of Viv's phone number and go around to his house. He greets me wearing a vest made out of the stars and stripes! Then he plays (Bonzo LP) *Gorilla* for me, and asks me to see their show, which I did. I later phoned him back, saying that I wanted in. Little did I know what I was in for! Me, this poor little jewish kid from Beverly Hills. I remember rehearsing at Raymonds Review Bar (featured in The Bonzo's appearance in the Beatles' film, *Magical Mystery Tour*). I recall learning the tunes, and eventually going out on the road— all of this in about two weeks! I didn't have any idea who, or what, I was getting into. All I knew is that I seemed to get along with the guys and fell into the concept of what the band was doing.'

Like most of the British pop bands of the time, they attended art college: Smith and Stanshall at Central London, Ruskin-Spear at Ealing (with The Who's Pete Townshend), Innes at Goldsmiths, and Slater at St. Martin's. Their interest in art can be seen in the original name for the band: The Bonzo Dog Dada Band (named after the anarchic Dada art movement of the 1920s). Stanshall: 'For a start we were to be called The Bonzo Dog Dada Band, but then we decided that nobody had ever heard of the word, or knew what it meant. We changed it to 'Doo-Dah' because we'd heard a lot of people use the word, saying: 'Where's the doo-dah?', meaning something that you couldn't put your finger on. We didn't want to be limited.' (Bonzo Dog itself was from a famous cartoon strip of the late '20s, created by George E. Studdy.)

Bonzo first met Python in early 1968 when the band threw in their lot with Terry Jones, Michael Palin, Eric Idle and Terry Gilliam to present the television extravaganza *Do Not Adjust Your Set* for the British Rediffusion TV network. 'Legs' Larry Smith remembers the young future Pythons fondly: 'They were a damn sight straighter than we were. They were like students to me. It was just like working with students again - we'd only been students ourselves two years ahead—but they were a lot straighter, a lot more disciplined. They hadn't had the exposure we'd had of a couple of years on the road doing tours and stuff. Obviously, it was their show, so they had to behave themselves and be a little more responsible than us.'

The Bonzo's approach to television was anarchic. They would do anything that was stupid, from wearing grotesquely oversized rubber heads to dressing up in a seal costume and presenting 'the seal of good housekeeping.' But the children loved it (after all, it was mainly a kid's program and the studio was packed with them). But the surprise came when it was discovered that it was their parents who came rushing home from work to catch the madness. 'It must be a program for super-intelligent kiddies,' Stanshall quipped at the time. 'Why else would they put us on at half-past five in the evening?'

Aside from contributing songs to the show, the Bonzos also appeared in sketches, usually odd, silly things like the one called 'Highlights From The Table Tennis Match: Remember This Exciting Moment?' and the camera would show 'Legs' Larry Smith collapsed over a ping pong table. The series is also remembered for a serial called 'Captain Fantastic and Mrs. Black' which became so popular that it was later developed into a series in its own right. (The character of Captain Fantastic was played by series regular and knock-about comedian, David Jason. His presence on the show irked Terry Jones somewhat as he felt he was a perfectly good knock-about comedian.)

Unfortunately for the Bonzos (who were constantly on tour), their participation in *Do Not Adjust Your Set* required them to take long overnight train journeys into London in order to film (read *DO NOT ADJUST YOUR SET: A Hygienic View by 'Legs' Larry Smith* for his account). Joel Druckman: 'An average day on tour with the Bonzos would mean getting up, smoking hash, and looking for chicks, practicing songs, playing gigs in the evening, where we'd smoke more hash, look for more chicks and have lots of sex.'

The strain was becoming tremendous, and road madness eventually began to infiltrate their personal lives as well. 'Legs' Larry Smith: 'I remember strange rehearsal rooms and odd places in Hobarth... fairly boring, dismal rooms where all this madness would be rehearsed. I wish we'd been in a healthier state, physically and mentally, to have done the TV series. But the show worked. It was bloody funny and it's still well-loved by a lot of people.'

A lot of the fun evaporated midway through the band's second American tour, in 1969. This translated into long tours across the States with crippling schedules and ever-decreasing communication with their management. Joel Druckman: 'We played so much that, after a while things started to get really weird. I remember riding in the band car and we stopped to pick up this hitch-hiker. I told the others to follow my lead and I start telling this poor guy how I'm really into weight-lifting and stuff. You know, the whole Mr. Apollo trip (later the nucleus of the Bonzo song of the same name), and all the time I'm taking off my clothes. Then we stop the car and I get out and pick some flowers and I start to eat them! And this guy is freaking out! Madness... Absolute madness.'

Although they were the critics' darlings, and well-respected by their peers, the Bonzos never caught fire commercially in America. Although they came close. They were just about to crack the U.S. market when the strain of it all buckled them to their knees. Bad management and a series of personal tragedies forced the band to abandon a potentially lucrative shot on American Bandstand and a coast-to-coast show. 'Oh it just really pissed me off,' says Smith. 'We were really starting to go down well. We were blowing people like Steve Miller off the stage. We practically blew the Grateful Dead off stage on our very first show in Boston.' (The infamous Boston Tea Party show in 1967.) The group soon disintegrated and slumped back to Britain to play one last gig at London's Lyceum Theatre, in January 1970. Smith: 'It just didn't happen for us. We hadn't yet reached the age of today's global exploitation - which we'd loved to have been a part of. Today we'd have been perfect.'

Of the Pythons, it is Eric Idle who most acknowledges the contributions that the Bonzos made to Monty Python. Neil Innes: 'Eric acknowledges that working with the Bonzos in the early days sort of gave him the idea about his anarchistic approach to comedy, one which Python sort of controlled in television and were very successful at. A lot of people think you go on television and just muck about, but you don't. To do that stuff it has to be carefully worked-out.'

The roots of Bonzoism run silent and they run deep. Their inspiration and influence can be seen and heard in dozens of bands, ranging from Was (Not Was) and The Art of Noise, to a little-known Liverpudlian band called Half Man / Half Biscuit. Bonzo fans run the gamut, from classically trained keyboard wizards like Rick (Yes, The Strawbs) Wakeman to folkies like Richard Thompson. Boy George, Jeff Beck, John Cale, Gene Pitney, Elton John, Eric Clapton, the Residents, Negativland, They Might Be Giants, Frank Zappa, Wreckless Eric, Jarvis Cocker, Captain Beefheart, Steve Winwood, Joe Cocker, and the Beatles all count themselves as fans. And, of course, so do the Pythons. 'Legs' Larry Smith: 'I'm sure we helped Python to carry on as much as they helped us to realize there are mad people about in this world - and you know, it's rather nice when you meet.'

Not a pretty sight.

THE MYSTERY OF "THE WEE-WEE SKETCH"

As we have learned, throughout the checkered history of *Monty Python's Flying Circus,* censorship (or the menace of censorship) was a constant concern; a 16-ton weight that hung over their heads and threatened to drop on them at any moment. We have seen incidences where sketches were nearly censored by the group (Terry Jones' concerns over "The Undertakers Sketch"), sketches that were censored by members of the group (Terry Gilliam's self-censorship of his own "Crucifixion / Telephone Pole" cartoon in series one), and sketches whose blow was needlessly softened by BBC censorship (taking out the word "masturbating" in "The All-England Summarize Proust Sketch", and substituting the word "gangrene" in the Gilliam cartoon about the prince who develops a spot). But, there is even a case where an entire sketch was not only censored, it has disappeared entirely: "The Wee-Wee Sketch".

Although the writers of the sketch in question are in question (Eric Idle believes that he wrote it with Michael Palin, while Graham Chapman also claimed credit), what is known is that it was developed around the end of the third series and involves a wine tasting. In the sketch a steward offers a man a glass of what he says is a premium wine. The man takes a sip and is then asked what he thinks of it. The man then goes into a long pontification about the wine, it's vintage, what sort of soil it was grown in, the climate of the area and so forth. "Am I right?" the man asks smugly, to which the steward casually replies, "No sir, that's wee-wee." The man is then offered another glass from another bottle and the scene virtually repeats itself ad infinitum.

While the sketch may not have been in the best of taste (literally), it was hardly as daring as "The Undertakers", nor as morally reprehensible to the BBC as "Ypres 1914" (Python's supposed mockery of World War I), so why then was "The Wee-Wee Sketch" cut, and by whom? It has been suggested by some (even by Idle) that John Cleese was so disgusted by the skit that he went behind the backs of the other Python's and personally requested that the BBC's Head of Light Entertainment (Bill Cotton) and the Head of Comedy (Duncan Wood) axe it. While there is possible merit to this theory (Cleese's distaste for toilet humor is well-known), John did participate in an equally distasteful sketch in the third series called "Blood Donors" where Idle played a man who wanted to donate urine instead of blood.

Whether John personally appealed to the Powers That Be or not, the sketch was listed in the BBC's infamous "Thirty-Two Points of Worry" memo as being one prime for the cutting room floor (although no copy of that letter seems to have survived to back this claim up), and the sketch did not appear in any episode of *Monty Python*.

In recent years, an even more intriguing theory has developed which suggests that the sketch was scripted, but never filmed. And, even odder, there are even those in Monty Python who disagree: some of the Pythons are certain that the sketch was filmed, while others don't remember shooting it at all (David Sherlock vividly recalls seeing a video of the sketch). So what then is the answer? What happened to "The Wee-Wee Sketch"?

One possible answer lies with the late Graham Chapman. Many years after Python, Graham began a new career touring American colleges talking about his life in and out of Python. During the course of the show he would feature a Q&A section, and would occasionally be asked about this sketch. Graham would then go into great detail about it, casting himself as the steward and (usually) Eric Idle as the hapless customer who drinks the wee-wee. However,

Graham would also do something else: he would supply the punch line. So here, for the first time anywhere, is a (the?) punch line to the infamous "Wee-Wee Sketch":

After several glasses of wee-wee, the Steward offers the Man one more. The Man reluctantly takes a sip - then spits it to the floor in disgust.

STEWARD: How did you find *that* wine, monsieur?

MAN: That one tasted like shit!

STEWARD: Ah! I see you're developing a keener palate!

Ringo Starr and
Peter Sellers in a
tender moment.

A SCOTSMAN ON A HORSE: IAN MACNAUGHTON ON PYTHON

Interestingly, not a lot has been said either by, or about, director Ian MacNaughton and his work with Monty Python. In much the same way that the Beatles had producer George Martin to help make some of their more freaky musical ideas work, the Pythons were fortunate to have a kindred soul of this veteran director at the helm. MacNaughton had been personally chosen by the Pythons themselves (especially Terry Jones) due to his work directing Spike Milligan's seminal Q series. Graham Chapman: "Ian had a spark of craziness about himself which we appreciated, and which made him appreciate the bits of idiocy that even some of us thought were too idiotic to do! So that was quite good."

Unfortunately, due to previous commitments on his part, Ian did not actually direct the first four episodes of *Monty Python* (although he did direct the filmed portions). The directing duties for the studio portions of these four episodes fell instead to a director named John Howard Davies. According to Chapman, the two directors were very different in style: "John Howard Davies was more clinical and formal and very efficient while Ian gave an atmosphere of being in it and chaotic. But Ian was, nevertheless, efficient as well. Not a lot of credit for the success of the *Monty Python* series has been given to Ian MacNaughton, which is a shame really, as Ian was a jolly fellow to work with."

MacNaughton was not only responsible for seeing that the shows were produced on time, and on budget, but he was also the point man between the team at the BBC, often taking the heat when things went wrong. However, contrary to many others, MacNaughton does not remember the series having many problems with the higher-ups at Broadcasting House. In a recent interview with BBC Radio he said: "The truth is, a lot of people at the BBC liked (the series) and also a lot of people couldn't understand why people liked it... I knew why people liked it because it was funny... and it still is."

He does, however, recall receiving some flak regarding the show's name: "After eight episodes had been shown, I received a letter from a Brigadier somebody-or-other and in this letter the Brigadier said: 'I am very disappointed with your series. I have watched eight episodes and I have seen no flying and not one single circus act!'" And although many of the show's sketches refer to the BBC establishment, MacNaughton's view is that many gentleman in "high establishment positions" lay themselves open for jokes and comedy at their expense. "Of course," he adds, "we never meant it nastily." But did MacNaughton ever worry that they had gone too far with any of the sketches? Macnaughton: "No!"

MacNaughton's memories of working with the Python team are generally pleasant ones with little or no discord: "My worst memory of working on Python was any day that we needed clear skies and sunshine I always stood in the rain... and my best memory is the fact that at the end of every day's shooting, we were all still friends." Ian and Graham Chapman were especially close on location. Chapman: "Location filming was usually a matter of long stretches of complete boredom occasionally broken-up by short periods of intense activity, and Ian and I could often be found spending many pleasant hours in some local hotel bar marinating our brain cells. Ian and I shared a common bond in our great love affair with ethanol. Usually all it took was him saying, 'Hey, hen, how about a drink?' and soon one drink would lead to the inevitable tray!" However, Chapman did feel that Ian's matey countenance didn't jibe well with everyone in Python. "I think John was especially put-off by Ian's tendency to be overtly friendly."

However, 30 years on, Ian MacNaughton says he'd do it all over again: "I would have continued directing *Monty Python*, but we all felt that it was better to stop when we were at a peak than to run the risk of winding down. I feel very happy—not proud—just happy, that people today are just as silly as I was."

OTHER PYTHONIC READING MATERIAL

If you've enjoyed this book, and would like to read more about Monty Python, its members and their times, why not ring Mr. Griffiths of Mayfair? He will be delighted to show his collection of rare prosthetic devices and Monty Python memorabilia. Or, you could read these fine books instead:

GRAHAM CRACKERS: FUZZY MEMORIES, SILLYBITS AND OUTRIGHT LIES, by Graham Chapman and Jim Yoakum
Career Press, 1997 (U.S.)
ISBN 1-56414-334-1

THE MONTY PYTHON ENCYCLOPEDIA
By Robert Ross
B. T. Batsford Books, 1997 (U.K.)
ISBN 0713482796 (paperback)

THE LIFE OF PYTHON: THE HISTORY OF SOMETHING COMPLETELY DIFFERENT, by George Perry
Running Press Book Publishers, 1995 (U.S.)
ISBN 1-56138-568-9 (paperback)

THE FIRST 20 YEARS OF MONTY PYTHON
By Kim "Howard" Johnson
St. Martin's Press, 1989 (U.S.)
ISBN 0-312-03309-5 (paperback)

FROM FRINGE TO FLYING CIRCUS: CELEBRATING A UNIQUE GENERATION OF COMEDY (1960-1980), by Roger Wilmut
Eyre Methuen, 1980, 1982 (U.K.)
ISBN 0-413-50770-X (paperback)

MONTY PYTHON: COMPLETE AND UTTER THEORY OF THE GROTESQUE,
Edited by John O. Thompson
British Film Institute, 1982 (U.K.)
ISBN 0-85170-119-1 (paperback)

MONTY PYTHON: THE CASE AGAINST,
By Robert Hewison
Grove Press, 1981 (U.S.)
ISBN 0-394-17949-8 (paperback)